MARCH TO ARMISTICE

MARCH TO ARMISTICE 1918

Christopher Haworth

WILLIAM KIMBER

First published by
WILLIAM KIMBER & CO. LIMITED
6 Queen Anne's Gate, London S.W.1

© 1968 William Kimber & Co. Limited
SBN 7183 0151 X

This book is copyright. No part of it may be reproduced in any form without permission in writing from the publishers except by a reviewer who wishes to quote brief passages in connection with a review written for inclusion in a magazine or newspaper or a radio broadcast.

MADE AND PRINTED IN GREAT BRITAIN BY PURNELL & SONS, LTD.
PAULTON (SOMERSET) AND LONDON

DEDICATION

To the Argyll and Sutherland Highlanders, a famous fighting regiment; to all fallen comrades; and in memory of all who served their country on land, sea and in the air.

CONTENTS

		Page
	Preface	11
	Historical Notes	12
1	Reveille	13
2	Draft	21
3	Adventure	29
4	Winizeele	49
5	Gloria	60
6	The Parson and his Parish	71
7	Preparation	87
	Historical Notes	99
8	The Beginning of the End	100
9	Loving Your Enemy	112
10	The Victory March	129
11	We Will Remember Them	146
12	Armistice	161

Maps

The Ypres Front in April 1918	9
The Advance in Flanders, September–November 1918	10

ILLUSTRATIONS

	Page
Transport passing the ruins of the Cathedral and Cloth Hall of Ypres in 1917	33
Troops moving up the line—the light railway near Ypres	34
Ration party	34
Working party going out at night	51
A 9.2 railway gun about to open fire at nightfall	51
Inniskillings of the 36th Division advancing in Flanders, September 1918	52
The Argylls crossing a railway, October 1918	85
The battlefield of Ypres in 1918	86
Troops on rest behind the line	86
An observation balloon on Pilckem Ridge	103
Digging wounded out of a collapsed regimental aid post	103
Artillery observation post near Ypres, August 1918	104
Limbers held up by mud on the Menin Road and supplies transferred to pack-mules, 29th September 1918	121
RAMC and German prisoners attending to the wounded	122
French cavalry resting in 29th Division lines, unable to advance further	122
Outpost of the Argylls on the Lys Canal	139
Captured German 5.9 near the Menin Road	139
Argylls crossing the Lys, 18th October 1918	140

All the illustrations listed above are reproduced by courtesy of the Imperial War Museum

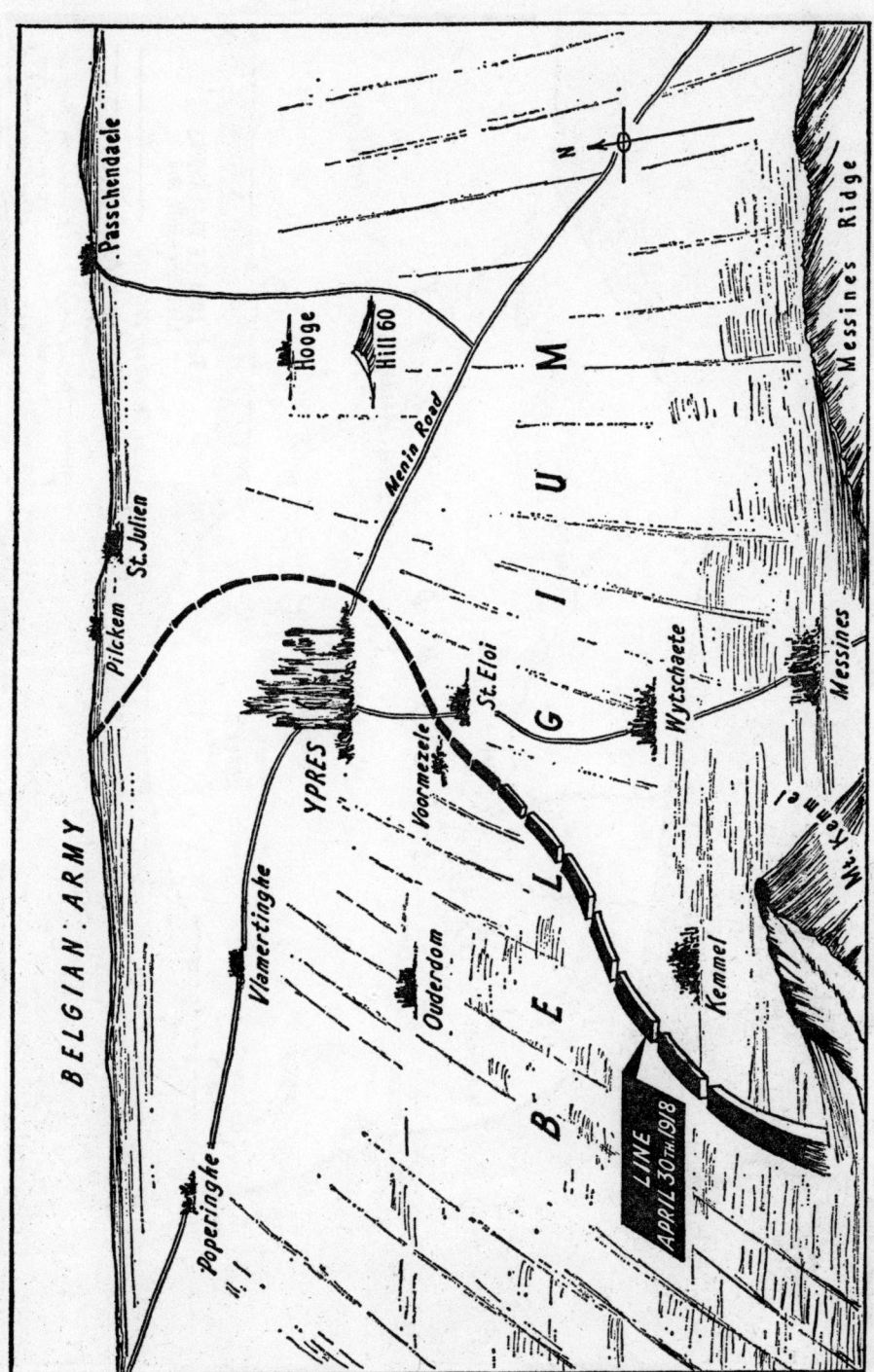

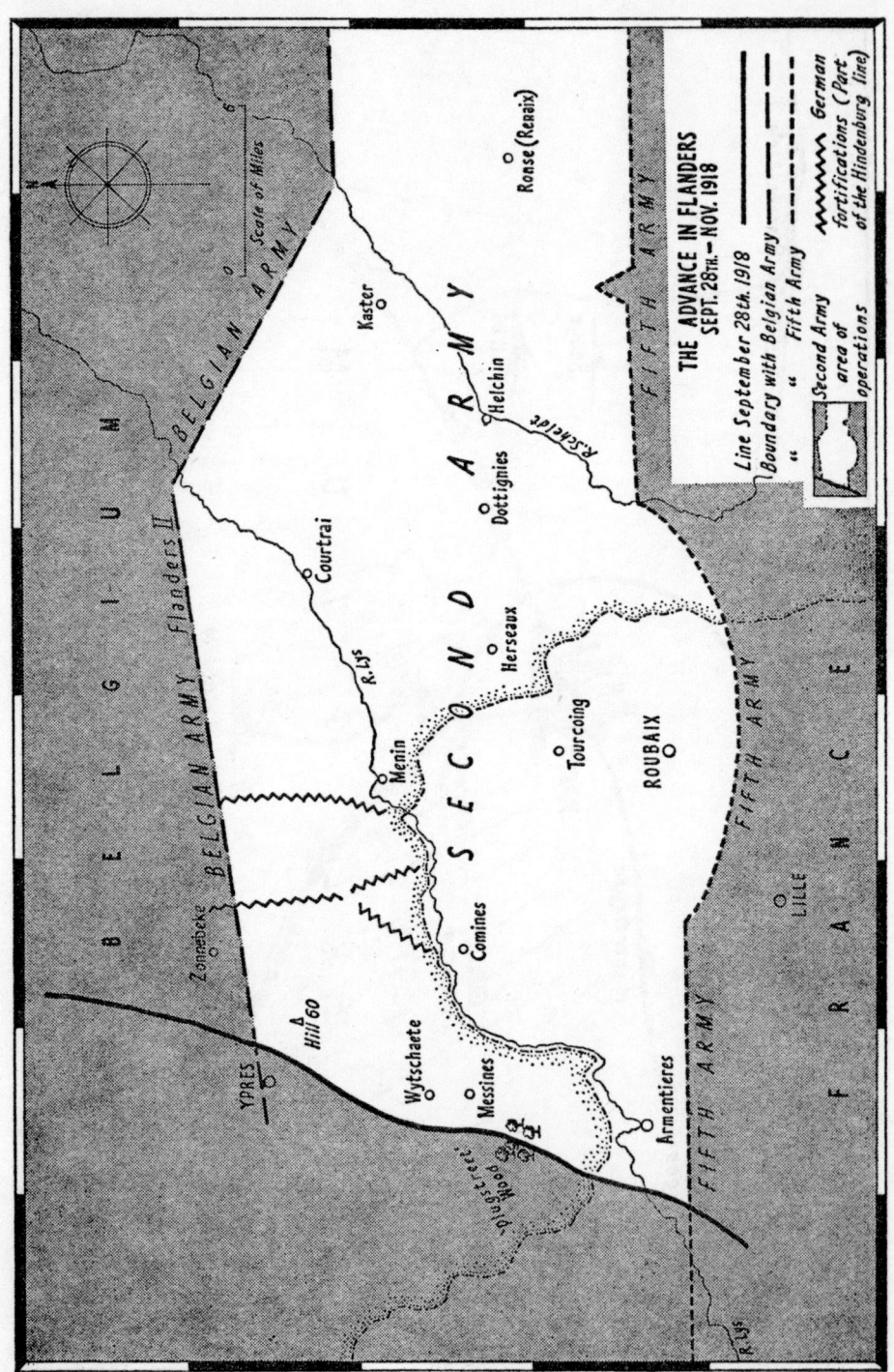

PREFACE

This is an account of the concluding phase of World War I being the impressions of a Private soldier. The incidents were recorded in diary form at the time of happening and extended during the first week after the Armistice on 11th November 1918. Later it was set down in narrative form and has reposed in my desk over the years; being factual, it has not been coloured by the imagination of later years.

I left school in 1913 at the age of 14, and when war was declared on 4th August 1914, I had served one year as an apprentice Law Writer. My father was in the RAMC and his brother was a Sergeant serving in France from 1915 until his death in action in 1918.

In 1916 at the age of seventeen, I formally enlisted and received my first day's army pay, and on my 18th birthday on 8th May 1917 I reported for duty and was sent to a Training Reserve Battalion.

Personal experiences of the war were related to me on my visits to father at a Second Western General Hospital where I conversed with the nurses and the wounded. I also heard regularly from Uncle John in France (he had been awarded the DCM) who kept me in the picture as far as letters could, and offered advice. His first hint was: 'Always obey orders and not much harm will come your way' and 'Learn to be a good soldier'. He was mortally wounded and taken prisoner during the retreat of March 1918 and died in Germany; thus, at the age of nineteen, I was to take his place.

I arrived in France under Number 29366 as a reinforcement to the 14th Argyll and Sutherland Highlanders in the 14th Division. They had been bitterly cut up (as were all our Divisions) during the German Spring Offensive.

Ypres was 'quiet' when I arrived, the enemy having run his course and was held, although now on the very outskirts of the martyred city.

I quickly became aware of at least one deficiency of the British Army: no watches. None were issued and added to this, my wristlet watch expired at Etaples. My platoon possessed a single watch but I do not recollect who was the owner. The acting Captain—an outstanding fellow whom I admired for his calm approach and leadership on patrols—had a watch which he kept in a tobacco tin. In the line he wore the uniform of a private soldier, a sensible precaution.

My notes, 'The Western Front 1918', the 'Second German Offensive in 1918' and 'The Final Advance 1918' are based on reading *A Short History of World War I* compiled by Brigadier-General Sir James E. Edmonds, C.B., C.M.G., a masterly work. The Brigadier's account covers almost a hundred pages as compared with my brief notes for the phraseology of which I alone am responsible.

I am deeply grateful to my daughter, Margaret, for reading the script and to her friend, Miss Joan Smith of Wolverhampton, who so kindly typed the manuscript.   C.T.H.

THE WESTERN FRONT 1918

The beginning of 1918 found the Western Front short of infantry, as sufficient drafts had not been provided to replace casualties. With fewer men, the British Army had to take over a bigger responsibility and the German Army was preparing to attack either in February or March before the Americans were able to throw any strong forces into battle.

The Germans struck on the 21st of March, the first offensive being in the Arras–St Quentin area. At 4.40 in the morning, in a thick fog, high explosives and gas shells crashed upon the British lines.

Wearing gas masks in fog restricted the visibility to between ten and twelve yards, but the British held their position, offering stout resistance. Communications were cut, making it impossible to call for artillery support, and the troops had to rely upon their own shooting and the machine gunners; they remained unshaken and defended to the last, causing havoc among the enemy.

Beating off an attack in such strength was a terrible task.

By the 22nd March most of the battle line was lost. The German objective was to drive the British back to the sea and, as the days passed, more ground was lost.

On the 26th March, General Foch, by Allied agreement, was put in charge of the Allied Armies creating at last a unified command. The Supreme War Council now ceased to control operations.

On the 4th and 5th April the Germans made a final effort to reach Amiens and got to within nine miles of the town, but here they were checked by the British Fifth Army and then driven back by the Australians who had been brought in from the Second Army.

SECOND GERMAN OFFENSIVE IN 1918:
THE BATTLE OF THE LYS

During the night of 7–8th April the Germans pounded the British battery positions between Arras, the La Bassee Canal and Armentiéres with mustard gas, 30,000 to 40,000 shells falling in two sectors. The attack then fell upon three divisions of the Second Army who were in the line at half strength owing to the March battle. The prospect was gloomy and on 11th April 'Backs to the wall' was the order of the day. Since 21st March the British casualties had amounted to 210,000 men and reinforcements numbered only 114,000. The attacking Germans were cut down by furious machine-gun fire compelling them to return to their jumping off places time and time again suffering heavy losses. The British casualties had reached to nearly 250,000 by the 21st April but on the arrival of the French who put four Divisions into the Kemmel Sector, Plumer was able to pull out six weak and tired Divisions for a rest and re-fit.

On the 24th April the enemy captured Mount Kemmel and Plumer withdrew the main British line nearer to Ypres, but by the 30th April the German offensive had been brought to a standstill, the channel ports had not been reached. The Flanders front became quiet except for the usual bombing raids.

1

Reveille

On my 18th birthday, 8th May 1917, I became Private C. T. Haworth 29366 and was welcomed into, and clothed by, the army, being convinced by the NCO's of the depot that we should be proud and honoured to wear the King's uniform. The regular soldier wanted to get the war over quickly to enable him to get on with what he called 'real soldiering'. We wanted to get out to the front and not perform ridiculous drills and ceremonial parades. Thus the new army differed somewhat from the old regulars.

As winning the war was a job worth doing, something big, I had an interest and an aim, and felt that I would take to this life. Although I must keep my personality, I must adapt myself to a new kind of life, a new set of conditions. There would be some things I would dislike, but whatever it was I wanted to enter into the spirit and learn to be a good soldier.

We entrain for a Training Reserve Battalion, and on arrival are received graciously, after which the Sergeant Major and a sergeant bring tea and sausages from the cook-house. Swearing is forbidden in this camp, the officers and NCO's being specially selected, which helps considerably in bridging the gap between 'civvy street' and this new venture. My first Company Commander was Captain Britten, respected for his kind-heartedness. He was later killed in action. The regimental staff are a fine set of fellows who help considerably in making life worth while, for I doubt very much if any of the lads had been away from home longer than a holiday or Scout camp. Our greatest disappointment is that we have not been issued with a rifle, but a sergeant informs us that we may not like it when we do have one.

We pass on to another camp, more strenuous, and receive our heart's desire—a rifle—which we have to clean, carry about and perform arms drill with. The sergeant at the last camp knew a thing or two when he was questioned about a rifle. Still, we are happy and content and we love to amble to the village, some three miles away, at the end of the day. Sunday is the special occasion when we attend a church service, voluntarily, after which we retire to the hall to sing hymns informally and to receive free refreshments. On our pay of half-a-crown to three shillings a week we are not exactly sons of Croesus. The homely evenings are thoroughly enjoyed—the friendly atmosphere, the warm glow of kindly people, and the wonderful women helpers whose smiles charm away all gloomy thoughts (not that we have any). This harmonious friendship helps to maintain the balance of life, especially for one who leaves home for the first time. We feel that someone cares; an atmosphere of beauty and love is radiated by that wonderful congregation of women giving up their time to be such delightful hosts.

Our officers and NCO's are kindly and considerate. One of our sergeants was a member of St John's Ambulance and although he joined the RAMC now instructs us in the use of the rifle. Since he was wounded in France and is unfit for active service, he has been selected as Instructor. He instructs us unofficially in other things important to our inner self. Another notable person is the sergeant-major in charge of physical instruction: he bellows like the bull and pulls ugly faces, thunders at one erring recruit to 'run to the Orderly Room and whitewash the last post.' Off parade he is gentle and treats us like sons. The tallest man in the battalion, although only eighteen, is six feet two inches tall and caused considerable amusement when he joined, for he brought a large packet of study books in connection with a postal course of tuition. Ludicrous as it may appear, it is a stern reminder of the careers we should be pursuing instead of learning how to kill.

We move on to Wales, but my mind is not attuned to the beauty of the mountains, except perhaps on Sunday, as we are on duty for more than twelve hours a day.

Here I meet Sam Graham, as we occupy beds adjoining each other. Being ex-Boy Scouts we become fast friends. The boys, many of them Welsh miners, are very good companions but their vocabulary would turn green trees a sickly yellow if they had feelings. Sam and I make a mutual pact to refrain from swearing, which we keep—for three weeks—then we fall. We had become absolutely fed up with our daily exertions, and boiling over, without any warning, Sam releases a string of oaths.

'Thanks, Sam. I feel that way, too,' and I follow suit to relieve my pent-up feelings.

We are drafted to Ireland, having completed our training, and now we take up specialist work. Ireland is supposed to be hostile, but to our pleasant surprise we are welcomed by colleens waving from the quayside. We make the acquaintance of the C-of-E Garrison Chaplain who is Scoutmaster of the Curragh Troop, and volunteer to assist in the evenings. The Padre invites us to supper to talk over Scouting.

The time draws nigh; Sam and I take down our best uniform and polish our boots to perfection, whereupon our room-mates enquire: 'What's the big idea?'

'We're taking supper with a Captain,' we reply, and keep the boys guessing as to who the Captain may be. Our prestige is enhanced now that we are honoured to sup with a Captain.

The Padre's wife is an amiable hostess and entertains us royally, although the subject we come to discuss is forgotten: the talk is confined to stories of uncanny and almost supernatural happenings.

We take advantage of our 'late pass' and linger on to a late hour, and on our return to the barracks we find the other occupants of the room sleeping soundly, and we go to our beds quietly.

The next night we go out into the darkness looking for the banshee, a spirit whose wail portends death in the house. Fortunately we do not locate our objective, whatever it might be, for nobody appears to have seen this mythical being even in imagination.

We do not suffer pangs of disappointment as a result of our fruitless search after the supernatural, but do feel hungry; our parcels from home, and postal orders, are not due until later in the week. I must say that we would not have the enjoyment of supper if a postal order or parcel did not arrive regularly from home, for the sum of three shillings a week does not go far these days, especially considering that out of this modest amount we must buy cleaning polishes, cigarettes, stamps and the usual personal requirements of youths of eighteen years' standing. Tonight the only possession Graham and I share is a penny stamp, and Sam looks glumly at me. I have an idea. I raffle the stamp, four fellows joining at a halfpenny each. It provides a measure of entertainment, and we increase our joint allowance to twopence; but how to buy supper for two out of a capital of two coppers? I go over to the canteen and purchase two penny slices of bread-and-butter (we call the substance butter from force of habit: actually the civilian population receive a ration of an ounce of butter each week) which I raffle among our friends at a halfpenny a chance. Out of this transaction we net the goodly sum of sixpence which provides a supper for Graham and myself consisting of a cup of tea and cake, and a packet of Woodbines each.

I am very happy in Ireland, and although the people are in a measure hostile to England, I find them extraordinarily easy to get on with. If there is animosity it is towards our government, and we are treated with the utmost courtesy and consideration, so much so that many of our fellows take a trip to Dublin on Saturdays and Sundays to meet their particular colleens.

The training is not so intensive, and altogether we are having a better time than when in Wales. We have a good Brigadier, and our officers are all that can be desired. On Wednesday afternoons we play games, and when the races are being run at the Curragh Racecourse we are free to attend.

Graham and I go to watch this sport of kings on one occasion and are astounded at the number of golden sovereigns heaped upon the tables of the roulette stalls. All kinds of games and tricks are in progress—'Find the Lady' (guess which thimble the pea is under, and however carefully you observe the manipulations of the trickster, you are always wrong); place a needle in the fold of a doubled-up leather bootlace—which is not as easy as it appears; all of which are interesting. The grandstand is packed with red-capped Generals and khaki-clad officers interspersed with priests complete with collar fastened at the back of the neck, and just a few people in civilian attire.

We find ourselves once more standing at the roulette table complete with golden coins, and a man is winning pounds on a lucky colour. I stake a shilling on the wheels of fortune and lose, much to the amusement of Graham who has lost his only halfcrown on a horse which came in last. As we move away from the roulette table a sergeant informs us that the man in charge of the wheel can stop the thing just as he wishes by the simple process of breathing deeply and causing his fat stomach to rest lightly on the side of the table.

I join the Signal Section, and each Friday we lead the brigade

Reveille

route march. I enjoy these marches and, being at the front of the column, the air is always fresh.

One particular Friday we are marching with an easy swing, keeping step with the bugle band behind us, when 'gas shells' are thrown by the General and his staff who are hiding on the other side of the hedge. The gas shells are made of brown paper containing a substance which sends out clouds of harmless smoke; we halt immediately and put on our gas respirators. During this action the band keeps on playing, not troubling to use their respirators, and the General jumps over the hedge, much displeased, and tells the bandsmen in strong language that they are all gassed.

I am now to leave my friend, Sam Graham, as I am transferred to the Royal Scots Fusiliers who are encamped at the Kildare end of the Curragh. My company is composed of boys under nineteen years of age, all of whom have been out in France. Many of them wear 'wound stripes', and one fellow of seventeen has three, having been first wounded at the early age of sixteen. The wound stripes are pieces of gold thread about an inch and a half long, and the soldier is entitled to wear one for each time he has been wounded. These young boys joined up giving a false age which was never questioned, and now they have been returned from France under a new army order which does not permit a soldier to go to the front under the age of nineteen.

The Signal Section claims me again, and one morning we are out on the Curragh, 'flag-wagging.' It is a bitterly cold day, and the velocity of the wind has almost reached hurricane force. We are the only people out of doors, but have only come into the open for half an hour after performing exercises with the 'buzzer' in the warm atmosphere of the YMCA hut.

The General on his chestnut mare gallops over the great plain, heading towards us and, as he approaches, reins in his horse, and orders the officer to take us indoors at once, saying it is not fit to have men out on a day like this. Yet the General has braved the elements, and it is thoughtfulness of this kind which men appreciate.

After a pleasant time spent under ideal conditions we are ordered to move to Scotland, and I go up to the old barracks and spend an evening with Graham prior to my departure.

With many regrets we steam out of Kingstown Harbour early in February, 1918, and after a rough crossing, plus a tremendous excitement caused by the close proximity of the German submarines, eventually leave our escort of destroyers and sail into Holyhead Harbour none the worse for our adventure, although a few of the men are looking a greeny colour.

After a sojourn in Scotland I travel south to join the Argyll and Sutherland Highlanders who are stationed on the Kent coast.

In the great expanse of sea and countryside I feel delightfully fit, and it is here that the coastal batteries engaged the German raiders who fly over at high altitudes on their journey to bomb London.

In the meantime my old battalion in Ireland has been drafted into France, and I receive word that my friend, Sam Graham, has been wounded and is in hospital in London. I obtain permission to visit him, and find he is suffering from 'trench feet' but having the time of his life in hospital where the nurses call him 'baby' as he is the youngest patient in the ward. It is a great experience to see him once again, but I am saddened when Graham mentions the names of boys I have known, and relates how they have been killed.

'What happened to "Darkie John"?' I ask. He was a swarthy lad of eighteen, from Wales, a miner with a heart of gold and a simple loving worship of his comrades who adored him. Having received but a scanty education he was childishly simple in his ways, and not being able to read well, he missed the pleasure and profit to be derived from books. Starting work in the coal mine at the age of thirteen, and living in a village where all the inhabitants were miners with the necessary sprinkling of shopkeepers to supply the needs of the working fraternity, his outlook on life was rather cramped, and until he joined the army less than a year ago had never been away from home and consorted with men of other occupations and ideas.

He loved his fellow men in the platoon, but was out of his environment as a soldier, for soldiering, as the Army Command looked upon it, was not in his line, and in that respect he would never make a good soldier, or should we say a *smart* soldier. He did not lack pluck and courage, and was no shirker where hard work was concerned: give him a pick and shovel and he would dig a trench far more quickly and evenly than twelve men like myself, but warn him for a general inspection, and he would almost weep.

The 'Defaulters' Call' was superimposed on the mind of Darkie John and he responded to that call of servitude in much the same way as a tired tram horse would to the ring of the bell. He was chained to something bigger than his simple mind could cope with, and however much he wriggled in those chains he could not rid himself of the yoke: strain as he would, the reins held him fast, yes, and hurt him. A defaulters' parade was never complete without him, and the tiresome servitude of extra fatigue duties took up all his spare time. It appeared that the gods had a grudge against the unhappy fellow, for he was unhappy, knowing he had always done his utmost to dress properly as becomes a smart soldier.

Each time Darkie John came before the Company Commander, the Captain would look unhappy, would sympathise and on occasion overlook punishment in the hope that Darkie might do better for himself and the honour of the platoon.

'Do you remember how we used to help him to dress?' laughed Sam, then more seriously: 'We left him in Ireland. He failed to pass the doctor, so perhaps he is better as he is. I don't want to go back to the front again. It's all blooming bunkum about fellows wanting to get better quickly in order to get out again. Believe me, it's no holiday out there.'

We talked on. The chaps I knew in the old Training Battalion. The tubby fellow always hungry: the first to be killed before they ever reached the line said Sam. The lance-corporal receptionist to the Medical Officer who invited some of the lads to visit the surgery in the evening and dispensed medicine when they had been turned away by the doctor at the sick parade that morning. That Sunday in Ireland when, to the sound of a military band, we hurried down a side street only to come face to face with a company of De Valera's men. Sam instinctively saluted and the salute was returned by their leader as the Sinn Fein army marched happily on.

I left Sam in the care of his glamorous nurses.

One of my newly found friends is a man of about thirty years of age, one of Kitchener's 'First Hundred Thousand' who in private life is a church organist. Edward Patterson has taken upon himself the task of fathering two other young fellows and myself, and we call him affectionately by the name of 'Uncle.' He not only tells us what to expect in France as regards the fighting, but prepares us for another side of life, that of women.

Being a married man and happy with his partner, he speaks

highly of them, but warns us about the type of women we might expect to meet on the other side and in fact here in England. He knows the history of this place and the surrounding district intimately, and on our walks together in the evenings, colours the conversation with stories of the past.

In the early evening we have just enjoyed a dip in the warm sea, the sun is shining and the white cliffs of France are to be seen in the distance, which makes us realise how close we in England are to the scene of activities on the Continent. Patterson suggests we take a walk to Sandwich, that quaint old Cinque Port of tortuous streets and ancient houses.

On our return journey we walk by way of the St. George's Golf Course, and as the summer sun is westering, the quiet of this walk fills me with an inward calm. It is great to be alive.

2

Draft

Reveille has been sounded and I am sitting up in bed reading, for it is Sunday, which in the Army, except for the necessary routine duties and guard duties, is a day separated from the week-days. There is a certain distinction about to-day; it speaks of rest and freedom from irksome drills, but there is one small grouse and that is the compulsory church parade; many a soldier reporting sick on Sunday morning to escape the parade has been seen in certain churches and chapels at the evening services. Church parade this morning is not until ten o'clock, and I will have oceans of time after breakfast in which to clean up my belt and bayonet, buttons and boots, and not unlike the other fellows I am enjoying this freedom of bed one day out of seven long after the bugler has sounded the call to rouse.

I share a room with ten other men; it is a large room on the top floor of an hotel which has been commandeered by the government as a billet. There are modern windows on three sides of the spacious apartment, and from two sides one may view the sea front, with the lightship in the distance, and occasionally a destroyer flotilla lends added interest to the seascape, as the ships plough their way through the channel on coastal duty. From the other side one may gaze upon a plain, broken here and there by woods, and on the extreme left is Richborough which is connected with Flanders by a regular boat service.

The silence is broken by Patterson who calls across: 'Have you the time, Haworth?' and putting down the book I am reading, and glancing at my watch I answer: 'Nearly twenty past seven.'

'Thanks. I'll have another ten minutes. Might as well take advantage while the going's good.'

The door is suddenly opened, and I look up to find the Orderly Sergeant, Corporal Dulworth, standing, notebook in hand.

'Come on, you lazy louts, time you were up,' says the corporal cheerily, and continues: 'Any of these men here?' commencing to read out a list of names.

I am wondering what is about to happen now, for I have a presentiment that something much bigger than an ordinary fatigue is about to take place. With much anxiety I wait to hear 'Private Christopher Haworth' and at that moment my name is called, followed by more names until the list is exhausted.

'Now all you men who have just answered your names,' the corporal now speaks more seriously, 'report at Company Office at nine-thirty. You're all for draft—France.'

He leaves the room, which is buzzing with the excited chatter of the occupants. I feel a peculiar sensation in my throat, and although I realise it is a dangerous undertaking, I am happy to be included for have I not been looking forward to service in France since I joined up on my eighteenth birthday almost a year ago? At last I am to come face to face with the grim reality of war; I am to be put to the test, and my youthful exuberance overflows with the possibilities of the great adventure before me.

I get out of bed and dress, then go over to Patterson who does not appear to take the news with the same keenness as myself.

'What's the matter, Patterson?' I enquire. 'You don't seem too happy about it.'

'No,' he replies. 'I'm not glad. When I got my last wound I thought I had finished with that side for good. It's my wife I worry about. However, we must make the best of a bad job and hope for a speedy return to blighty.'

'It's a bit rotten,' I agree.

'Ah well, I'm going for a wash. Coming?'

After breakfast we are fitted with new kilts and equipment and in the afternoon parade for inoculation. After tea a party of four, Patterson, 'Bunny', 'Claud' and myself walk along the dunes to Deal, a sailors' town devoted to the sea and a strange mixture of old and new. After refreshments in a Sunday School used as a recreational centre for the troops established in the town, Patterson went to the piano and entertained us with pieces from the *Messiah* and from Bach. And we are going to fight the peoples of those great musicians who have given so much to the world.

Patterson leaves the piano and a Royal Marine asks him why he has been playing German music. In a kindly way Patterson explains that because of a quarrel with Germany we cannot challenge everything German. What of Schubert with his simple-hearted good fellowship with all people? Or Schumann the exemplar of faithful married love, and above all Beethoven?

The Royal Marine is astonished for he had considered it unpatriotic to play German music although he admitted his appreciation of Patterson's playing.

Monday morning we go on four days' draft leave, two days being spent in travelling to and from our homes; but we are more fortunate than many chaps who have gone to the front without having any leave.

I enjoy myself until departure time arrives when I feel a lump in my throat. People appear calm but a mask is hiding the all too obvious fears. The crowded train and the cheerful banter with relatives. The last farewell kiss.

Good-bye! A shrill whistle, and we are off.

The occupants of the compartment become acutely quiet. The train gathers speed and the sound of the revolving wheels dins into my head, *Over the top, over the top*. The clamorous sound will persist in singing, *Over the top*. It changes as the train proceeds. *Will you come back?* on and on, *Will you come back?* and the words are almost choking me, for I have as much certainty of escaping with my life as a condemned man. Will I ever see the old home again? Have I seen all my loved ones for the last time? And the sound of the wheels says, *Don't be too certain*. Oh, the mocking wheels, have they no brighter message?

The other occupants stir out of their lethargy, Woodbines are produced, and conversation comes like an angel from above to drive away our morbid thoughts. The voice of the wheels now proclaims a more confident note, *Don't be a fool—You will come back—All will be well!* One of the fellows returning to France is in a 'Pals' Battalion,* and amuses us with vivacious anecdotes of life in France.

'Our captain,' says he, 'ordered the sergeant to take out a patrol one night—we were on a quiet sector at the time. He wouldn't go out himself, and sat in his dugout waiting for the patrol to return. "Don't forget to bring back a piece of German wire," said the captain, in order to have evidence that the patrol had been out as far as the enemy lines. The patrol went down the trench and over the top, and on reaching the German wire,

---

* These were battalions raised from volunteers, mostly in the Manchester and Liverpool areas, in 1914.

found an unused coil waiting to be picked up. We picked it up and brought it back with us.

'At the back of our trench was an old disused sap, with a good dugout. This was seldom visited, and the patrol dumped the coil of German wire in the dugout. The sergeant then snipped off a piece which he took to the officer.

'The next night the sergeant was ordered to take out a patrol again, and collecting his men, went down the trench, into the sap, there to spend an hour chatting and smoking. Before leaving, the sergeant snips another piece from the coil of German wire, and reports to the captain that there was a little activity on the left but all quiet on our front, and the officer says: "Very good, and did you bring back a piece of wire?" The sergeant produces the piece he has snipped from the coil in the dugout.

'That went on every night, and the old man never knew we had a coil of jerry wire on our side!'

In such pleasant company the time passes swiftly, and as the train steams into Euston I have lost the uncomfortable feeling of despair, and with a stout heart continue the remainder of the journey.

We have been in camp over a week, during which we have tested our gas respirators in the gas chamber, thrown live bombs into the sea, practised night firing, wiring, and other things which we are expected to perform in France. The night before we are to leave these shores we have a dinner in town, and toast with Dry Ginger. Patterson, as leader of our youthful party, will not celebrate in anything stronger, for he says that if we enter the hotel tonight, the other fellows, out of misplaced kindness, would no doubt press us to take too much, and at all costs we must be sober on the last night in dear old England.

And so to bed.

Today has been one of excitement and hustle. This morning, for the last time, I had a dip in the sea. Farewells having been extended to men I shall never meet again except perhaps by accident, we parade in readiness for our departure. We stand to attention as the bugler sounds the Last Post, and as Lights Out is being sounded at ten-fifteen, the band heads us to the station.

Marching into the town we are met and followed by crowds of people and soldiers stationed here, bidding us 'God speed.' We entrain for Folkestone, and the Brigadier speeds us onward with the words: 'Keep your spirits up and your heads down!'

Draft

Detraining at Folkestone we march to billets and spend the few remaining hours before daybreak in sleep.

After a hearty breakfast and being armed with a bag of sandwiches and chocolate for the journey, we march to the boat, and although this scene has been enacted daily since 1914, crowds of people cheer, and flags are flown from almost every house leading to the docks. The ship steams outwards, and we give one long cheer as the white cliffs of the Motherland gradually disappear in the distance.

Disembarking at Boulogne in the heat of the afternoon sun, we are faced with a stiff climb to St. Martin's Camp on the hill. Costermongers are persuading us to buy pears at sixpence each, which are being sold in England for twopence.

'*Soldats Angleterre* plenty money—plenty big mug is Tommee *anglais*.'

A boy about ten years of age is following us, crying: 'Come and see my sister . . .' the rest of the remark being lost in the exclamations of members of the draft: 'So this is France! It's not us they welcome, but our money!'

We take our own time in ascending the hill under the scorching sun, followed by Madame, shouting: '*Bière une sheeling*.'

Sweat pours from our faces. We gasp, we thirst, and still Madame follows with '*bière*' in the hope that some of us will give up the mighty struggle and pay a shilling for her filthy concoction. The Rest Camp looms ahead and at last we are able to divest ourselves of the heavy kit and cool down.

We were disappointed with the catering arrangements at a Base with every facility, easy supply route and away from danger. Cooks and others were in abundant supply, not so the rations for the 'poor bloody infantryman.' In effect, we had to be made as miserable as possible for when in such a condition a fellow does not worry whether he lives or not. A happy soldier does not want to die and this looked like the start of our conditioning.

'The same old crowd of Base Wallahs,' comments Patterson. Men clinging to a cushy job to keep them from the front while they bully the poor devils going to fight for them. And all those delicate NCO's, the physical jerks instructors and footballers who could not abide the trenches.

But we had seen other things no less intolerable since landing. I was distressed when I passed one of the buildings on the dock and saw a party of German wounded waiting to be conveyed to hospital; I could not help but sympathise with the men I am supposed to hate. What am I to make of it all? I am not at all happy about this business, but the job has to be done, and the only course open is to fight on and finish war for ever.

After spending the night at Boulogne we entrain for Etaples. On the journey we experience much fun owing to the prehistoric French railway carriage we occupy. The seat is hardly wide enough to accommodate our persons, having apparently been designed for the frail forms of infants, and the parcel rack is too small and fragile to receive our packs: the only useful purpose I imagine it can serve is that of a handy receptacle for a workman's roll and butter. After many halts by the wayside, ostensibly for the purpose of keeping the line clear for the regular French train service, we eventually arrive at Etaples.

What a place it is! One huge railway siding with hundreds of cattle trucks waiting to transport British troops to the line; a cemetery containing the graves of many of our soldiers who have died in hospital; and now the gigantic camp itself. On one corner are the hutments of the military hospitals, and at the other side of the wood is the camp proper with hundreds of camouflaged bell tents which are to sleep between sixteen and twenty men plus equipment. The canteen, dining rooms, and recreational centres are wooden structures.

We sojourn here for three days, during which we go before a medical board, where Patterson is marked unfit and will not serve in a fighting unit; I am thankful this is so for the sake of his wife, although I shall miss his excellent counsel and companionship. By degrees our party is split up and assigned to different units requiring reinforcements. A final test is made of our gas respirators by passing through a gas chamber of highly concentrated gas. On returning from this test, we pass the kennels housing the dogs, hundreds of them, which are used in the forward area for carrying messages.

Etaples is honeycombed with passages and underground caverns excavated to provide protection from the long-distance bombing raids. I serve four hours in a tunnel passing bags of surplus chalk along the chain of men, two yards apart until they reach the open ground.

In the evening I toured the various recreation huts, the largest being 'The Church Army.' The Salvation Army run another and the Boy Scouts have a hut where old Scouts are invited to get

Draft

together. These wonder palaces are nearly always crowded, care is cast aside as one is irresistibly drawn into a whirling stream of human happiness. Youthful gaiety singing popular songs. Clatter of crockery and hearty greetings. All these men have learned the art of being gay at the right moment and this is their moment.

On my last evening, I visit the Church Army with three of my friends. This hut will hold over a thousand and having obtained your mug of tea and eats, if you are alone, you will not be lonely for long. Groups of men sit reading and writing. At the end of the hut hangs a large curtain which I discover later veils an altar and chancel complete with organ. It is Sunday, and soon the whole area is transformed into a hallowed cathedral.

The place fills to overflowing. Nurses, WAC's, officers and men, and the service is most impressive. During the singing of the last hymn, men going up the line are invited to kneel at the altar for a blessing. I join the procession to the chancel as the congregation sing:

May the joy of Thy salvation
  Be their strength and stay;
May they love and may they praise Thee
  Day by day.

The chancel fills up. Row upon row of kneeling men as the assembly behind are singing:

Father, Son and Holy Spirit,
  God the One in Three,
Bless them, guide them, save them, keep them
  Near to Thee.

The clear and expressive words of the Blessing, and the service ends.

Another day and the ground is covered with a heavy dew sparkling under the rays of the sun; after breakfast we collect our belongings and with full equipment march to the siding to entrain for the front. I occupy a cattle truck with twenty other men and as the truck is registered to carry thirty men or fifteen horses we are not overcrowded. The route is by way of Calais, but the scenery is not interesting. The train stops by a refreshment bar and we alight like pigeons released from a basket for we do not feel inclined to consume the ration of bully beef which has been provided for the journey.

As the train moves on, the conversation becomes topical until the slow-moving train comes to a halt at St. Omer and we jump out to stretch our cramped legs.

I sink into a doze as the train again moves off and I am awakened by John Fraser as the others prepare a meal. The country is now marked with ruined cottages caused by long-range shelling or by aircraft bombing and soon we arrive at Hazebrouck—a railway junction with a line to Poperinghe for the Ypres Salient.

The driver is in no hurry as we set off again and I am feeling weary of this slow motion. Someone produces a pack of playing cards and a hand at pontoon passes away the time, for we have exhausted our supply of tall stories and we are a bit fed up with singing.

At a small siding we stop for good: an officer is calling out 'Argylls!' and we march to a quiet old village surrounded with hop gardens. The sun is setting, and it is peaceful, the green fields being restful after the long journey. Bell tents have been pitched in a nice green field, and here the kindly officer tells us we will stay the night. In no time, an orderly appears with a quantity of fried bacon, bread and tea, and we settle down to the meal we have been hungering for.

We sleep beneath clean blankets. Everything is so still and quiet here and my wish is that I might abide here until the war ends.

It is almost noon when the officer conducts us to a light railway, sees us on the train, and wishes us the best of luck. It makes all the difference when one is treated with kindness and consideration by one in authority.

The light steam engine puffs away through hop gardens and eventually pulls up by a row of dug-outs at Poperinghe where we are loaded with tins of water.

We now pass shell dumps and stores of all kinds and then the steam engine is changed and a petrol engine takes on the load, a reminder that smoke can be seen by the enemy.

At Vlamertinghe we disentrain and a guide takes us to a small camp of half-moon shaped huts and in turn we enter the Orderly Room where the Quartermaster duly enters our particulars in his records.

3

Adventure

At Vlamertinghe we prepare for war. We are going in to the line at Ypres. All the articles of value that we can do without in the line have been placed in a small sandbag and left at the QM stores for our return.

We have missed the ration train up to Ypres and feel glad, for we are tired. I had an idea we would rest here the night and sleep in a Nissen hut, and the quartermaster thought the same, but now a message has come through calling for supports. Being a Scout, I always like to take bearings and dislike going into a strange place for the first time at night; whilst waiting I have been getting as much information as I can from the men here.

'Is it quiet up there?'

'Yes, fairly. But at Wipers it's never really quiet,' answers the man.

Another chap comes up and says: 'Be careful, Jock, a patrol of the . . . went out the other night and didn't return. Not a shot was heard; it seems they must have all been surrounded and taken prisoner.'

'How cheerful,' I reply. All the same it seems a bit of a tall story.

The guide arrives, and our party depart on foot. The guns are booming, and occasionally a shell bursts quite near, but after the first shock I become more used to the explosions, and the adventure is too interesting to cause any great alarm. As we approach nearer the line the shelling becomes heavier, but the Véry lights hovering in the sky—a wonderful spectacle—attract my attention as fireworks have always fascinated me. 'It looks as if we're surrounded by those lights,' I say to the guide.

'Nearly. They mark out the Salient, and they'll be going up all the night.'

Presently I feel fatigued, and wish for the line in order to rest.

We cross over a canal and rest on the other side. An artillery officer comes up to us and urges us on, as his battery is about to open fire. On our feet again we break into a double as we arrive at the corner of the Great Square of Ypres. The moon is up, and as we run through the square our shadows cast upon the ruins by the moonlight create an uncanny spectre. We continue along quiet and deserted streets, the buildings of which are in ruins, then stop by the wreck of a house not unlike the others we have passed, the debris piled up all around, but as my eyes become accustomed to the sight, I notice the place is barricaded with sandbags. The guide draws a blanket aside, and four of us are ushered in, then he lifts another blanket, but not before the outer blanket has been placed in position again, and we find ourselves in a room lit by candles. This is the company office, and the Sergeant-Major is sitting on a box, using another box for a table.

'The new reinforcements, sir,' explains the guide.

The Sergeant-Major smiles and asks us if we have been out before. 'You will go to Four Platoon, in support,' he tells us. 'You needn't trouble taking them tonight,' he continues, looking at the guide. 'It's too late, and anyhow they're on a patrol now. Take them to the Nissen hut across the road to the left—you know the one?'

'Yes, sir,' answers the guide.

'So you come from Glasgow,' remarks the Sergeant-Major to one of the fellows.

'Yes, sir.'

'Do you know me?' As the lad hesitates he continues: 'My name is Seddon. Played right half——'

'Oh yes, sir, I've seen you play hundreds of times.'

The Sergeant-Major laughs, saying he hopes we will see him play again some day, then bids us 'Good night.'

'Good night, sir,' we whisper as the guide parts the blanket curtain once again and escorts us outside where we are now waiting for the others to come out and join us. The Sergeant-Major having taken their particulars, they emerge into the open, and the guide takes us to the hut. Before leaving us he warns us not to make a light under any consideration, for we are under observation. I lay myself down on the damp ground, expecting to sleep, but a big gun is near at hand, barking away, and continues most of the night.

Adventure

At dawn, a guide appears and conducts us to the support trench, and for the first time, for me, I 'stand-to.' On mounting the fire step, I look in front for a glimpse of the Germans, but see, instead of the enemy, utter desolation—shell holes, mud, barbed wire, and beyond the front line, standing like sentinels, are two rows of shattered tree stumps marking the road which in better days has been a beautiful avenue of lofty trees.

Soon the clatter of feet along the duckboards is heard, and the officers appear and we are duly presented. Then Fritz says Good Morning just as the sun is rising above his lines. Corporal Edwards turns to me and shouts: 'It's all right, lad, nothing to get the wind up about; this is only the usual morning strafe. Keep your eyes skinned in case he does come over, but it isn't likely.'

The trenches and communicating trenches are made in a curious zig-zag: the straight bit in the trench which has a fire step is called a bay, and the part which juts back is a traverse, so that sections of men are separated by the traverses. The corporal instructs me in all this. 'When you see a "Minnie"* coming, get behind the nearest traverse as quick as lightning: that's what they're for.'

In spite of a year's training, all this is new to me, and I now find myself thinking more of the sunrise than of the enemy. What a gorgeous spectacle! But how out of keeping with this foreground of mud and wire.

The danger of an early morning attack being past, the order to 'Stand down' is given, and the corporal takes me to a dugout which I am to share with a man who has been with the company a month. I am attracted to the corporal: he inspires confidence, and appears not to be frightened of anything. The fellow in the dugout says he will 'drum up.'

'What d'you mean?' I enquire.

He growls nastily, causing me to retort angrily: 'Get on with your drumming up as you call it.'

Windwood mutters something about me being a 'Rookie' as he fixes a piece of four-by-two into his small oil can and lights the cloth. Judging by the time it will take to boil a mess tin of water, he might as well keep his bit of four-by-two for its proper use, that of cleaning his rifle.

Corporal Edwards calls us to his dug-out for the rum issue and

* *Minenwerfer*—a bomb thrown by a trench mortar, literally a 'mine-thrower'.

I take my mess tin, expecting a generous ration. The officer looks at my tin lid, then smiles as he hands me a tot the measure of an egg-cup. This is intended to keep out the cold.

Breakfast appears long before Windwood's appliance has boiled any water, and for most of the day we watch a succession of air-combats. Heavy shells of the 'coal-box' variety fall too near to make me feel at home although I am learning to judge by the whistle where the shells will drop.

At dusk, Corporal Edwards rounds up six men including myself saying: 'You are on patrol tonight.'

We have to capture some Huns for interrogation and I feel a little windy for I am not a brave fellow, but as the job has to be done, I might as well make the best of it.

Going out on to the road we halt in front of the officer who awaits us and addressing the sergeant enquires if all the men are volunteers; the sergeant replies: 'Yes, sir!' as if we were all eager to go creeping about No-man's-land.

The officer leads, followed by the sergeant, corporal and we six men in single file and crossing the road enter a communicating trench where we receive the password for the night. We tramp along, then a man in front misses the duckboard his foot slipping into the water. The chap following does the same, and I hear a whisper: 'We ought to be in the b—— navy, not here.'

What a complex network of trenches. We call them trenches, but in this waterlogged salient they are actually breastworks of sandbags. We climb up, walking over the high ground as part of the trench has been blown in, then back again into the trench. Arriving at the front line, we scramble over the embankment, when—*Ping!*—and 'Freeze!' as a Véry light sails over. Another *ping!* Now *Rat-tat-rat-tat* . . . *swish-swish-weeze-sees* . . . *spat* . . . *spat-spat-spat* as bullets from the enemy machine gun flop into the defences.

My hands cover my face. A curious action almost uncontrolled, a sort of telegraph 'Preserve your eyes.'

'Come on, boys,' whispers the sergeant and we follow a zig zag course through our barbed wire. Another Véry light. 'Freeze!' After several disturbances caused by the lights we arrive at a farm and I am told to wait until ordered to move.

This so-called farm is nothing but a heap of bricks and old tin cans, and if I move the slightest bit I disturb the tins and bricks, making a noise; not knowing how near I am to the

Transport passing the ruins of the Cathedral and Cloth Hall of Ypres in 1917

Troops moving up the line—the light railway near Ypres

Ration party

enemy, this causes great uneasiness. The heavy shells go over: *wobble, wobble, hum, hum, wobble,* then: *Bang, crash, thump* somewhere in the rear.

My hosetops cover my bare knees, as knees or a white face are very conspicuous in the dark. I am attacked by mosquitoes, millions of the little beggars are biting through my stockings, and the irritation is becoming almost unbearable, but I cannot move or I shall disturb these ruins and frighten the enemy, a thing which I would not do for the world. I am here to capture some Germans, but I am not particularly anxious and anyhow we have thousands of them behind the line and at home in England; our general is a hard man to please, and he wants them fresh tonight. The fireworks are going up all around us, a terrible storm is brewing for it is raining heavily; now it is lightning, and the sound of the guns is nearly eclipsed by the roar of the thunder. I am saturated, and as the lightning flashes, wire entanglements are made conspicuous, creating a weird and fantastic picture. My heart beats quickly as the form of a man is passing in front of me. Is it a tree? No! Another passes, and another.

'Corporal!' I whisper. No answer! 'Corporal, corporal—is the officer there?' Silence! Where are my companions? More forms creep by.

My brain is working fast. I wonder if a German patrol is surrounding us. The story I heard last night down at Details appears before my mind. Is this going to be a repetition of the incident of the vanishing patrol? I call a little louder, as I get no answer. God! What has happened? Am I alone?

My finger is on the rifle trigger: dammit, I do not know where I am, but if it comes to a fight I am going to have a shot if possible. A Véry light is fired by the enemy and sails over in front of me, illuminating a wide area; keeping perfectly still I survey the ground, but not a human creature is to be seen.

A German machine gun now starts firing and a reply is sent back from the British lines, causing more German machine guns to come into action, and now it looks as if a war is on, for the enemy artillery is bombarding our lines to blazes. A slight movement in front of me brings my heart up to my mouth and perspiration freely flows from my brow, but my fear is allayed as I discover the noise is made by a rat scampering over the ground looking for food.

I have now stood here for over two hours with nothing but my imagination, and that has not been very consoling. During part of the time I have been trying to figure out the position of our lines in case I am alone, but the circle of Véry lights confuses me. Suddenly I hear the crunching of feet over the debris, and before I have time to turn around, a hand is slapped upon my shoulder, giving me another fright. Hell, I think, am I caught unawares after all?

A familiar voice whispers, 'Come on,' and I fall in behind the corporal, and crawl on hands and knees until *Ping!*—this time one of our Véry lights goes up and the sentry challenges: 'Password!' and the sergeant answers; 'Cricket.' We climb over the parapet into the trench where I heave a sigh of relief.

'Phew! what a first night,' I murmur.

We are tramping along the communicating trench in the direction of the supports, and our artillery is strafing the enemy lines: I am thankful, for it will keep the enemy guns quiet until we cross over the road. It is a bad piece of road and already eight men have been killed on it in the early evening before we came out on patrol.

We come out on to the road, and arrive at last at the support trenches; after much difficulty, slipping and sliding in the mud, which makes me angry, I find my dugout.. The corporal informs me that the captain of B Company who was bringing in another patrol has been killed out in No-man's-land, and in the darkness his body has been lost, which means a daylight patrol must go out in the morning.

I crawl into the dugout to sleep in my wet clothes, but I find rest out of the question, as the rats are running over my face, which is extremely annoying. Windwood is asleep, lucky fellow, and as a rat touches my nose, I hit out with my fist, and missing the enemy, find Windwood's face instead.

'What the b—— hell's the matter with you?' he yells. 'Have you gone mad? I'll punch your b—— nose in if you do that again.'

I roar with laughter.

'Think yourself funny, do you, you b—— fool? I'll stop your laughing in a minute.'

I have never heard a man express his vehement feelings more violently, but it cheers me considerably, and perhaps I may be able to sleep better now.

It does not seem long since I came back from the patrol, but the corporal is now at the entrance to the dugout, calling 'Stand to!'

'What a war!' I exclaim, as I take hold of my rifle and get out of the dugout into the fresh morning air, which is colder than the atmosphere in the dugout, and that is not much above zero. My feet ache, and my tunic and kilt are still wet through. I enter the support trench feeling half asleep, chilled to the bones and wishing I had been born a girl. We await the dawn and another day of foolish mad war and hate.

This morning our artillery is giving support to the Belgians on our left, and on the right there is a terrific bombardment going on, but our part of the line is quiet.

'I wonder what old "Jerry" is thinking about now,' I say to the corporal.

'Preparing for us in case we go over, I reckon, just as we are ready for him.'

The order to 'Stand down' is given, and we leave the trench and go back to the dugouts to await breakfast.

'How many prisoners did you collect last night?' sniggers Windwood.

'Prisoners? I forgot all about that! I don't even know if we got any at all.'

'I suppose you were all too scared to look for any?'

'Perhaps the others will have something to say about that,' I retort. 'It's curious you weren't selected for the party, isn't it? Last night is past anyway, and I'm going to drum up. Have you any tea?'

'It's about time *you* got some tea,' says he.

'That's what I think. I'm pining away for a taste of my favourite refreshment. Where's that tea you say you have?'

He dives into his pack and extracts a small packet of tea, and I look round the trench and pick up an apricot jam tin and punch a few holes in the top. A piece of sandbag, two inches square is placed at the bottom of the tin and a stub of lighted candle put on its side for the fat to run over the rag. The heat soon boils a mess tin of water.

A couple of rats come nosing round, as tame as kittens but as big as cats; they resent intrusion into their domain. One spits as we throw a lump of earth but makes no attempt to move from its dainty tit-bit. I must look into this and bury all scrap tins. My pack once contained a bag of emergency ration biscuits but I find a hole has been eaten into the side, the rats leaving nothing but a few crumbs.

'If those rats had known how to use a tin opener, the bully beef would have gone as well,' I say.

Windwood grunts as the water on my improvised cooker comes to the boil. A brew in twenty minutes.

I take my tea to the corporal's dug-out where he is talking to Dewer about rats. Dewer is saying: 'Great things are rats, but what about "chats"? Rats live on scraps and dead men but the little grey-backed lice live on live men.'

Breakfast up and Dewer leaves to bring his mess tin and the corporal detains me enquiring: 'Were you all right last night?'

'I was scared at one time. I thought I was alone.'

The corporal explained that I was left at the farm covered by two of the patrol while the others scouted round. 'We thought it would get you used to things. We did expect Jerry to have a patrol out, but it didn't come off, so we found no prisoners after all.'

After a pause, he added: 'Always stick to me and there'll be nothing to fear.'

Breakfast over and two patrols go out, one to recover the body of the captain of B Company, and the other to capture some prisoners, if any are available this morning. I stay behind, and I am not sorry either, for I will hear all the news when the parties return.

Later a patrol returns with the body of the captain and report all is quiet.

My face is overgrown with fungus but old Fritz deliberately sent over a few 'Whizz-bangs' just as I had worked up a nice lather on my face. I did not use the razor but rubbed off the frothy soap with my towel.

The other patrol comes in, bringing four burly Germans as prisoners, and the general will be pleased. This patrol was led by an officer nineteen years of age, who has endeared himself to the hearts of the men he took with him by displaying great courage, although he is as timid as a kitten. I hear that they got through a gap in the enemy wire, that the officer entered a dugout where he found four Germans asleep, and asked them to surrender, which they did without any trouble. He held them at the point of his revolver, and brought them up to his men who covered them with rifles and bayonets; then as they left the enemy trench the officer loaded his revolver. I believe he has been recommended for the Military Cross, which he deserves, stout fellow.

It is now time to commence our 'night ops' and Corporal Edwards has warned me that I am going on a wiring party. The sergeant appears, and we fall-in and march to the road, where the officer inspects us, and the sergeant-major makes a note of the men who are going out, in case of accidents.

We cross the two roads, enter the communicating trench, and wind along, stumbling here and there at places where the embankment has been blown down by enemy shells. Now the party turn right, down 'Dragoon Alley' and the order is passed down the file, 'Last man stay behind and direct other party.' I am the last man and halt; in a few minutes, two Engineers come by and follow my party down Dragoon Alley. I continue to wait until I begin to feel uneasy, for it is not a pleasant experience to stand alone in a trench on a dark night. Anything might happen, and it is not comforting to think of the possibility of being wounded by a piece of shrapnel, with no help available. Suddenly I recollect I have not been given the password for the night, which increases my anxiety, and after an interminable time I hear the welcome patter of feet coming along the trench from the direction of the front line. A runner turns the corner stops dead, facing me, for he does not expect to meet anybody at this point. Instantly he covers me with his rifle and demands 'Password.'

'I don't know—wasn't given any,' I answer as calmly as possible, for I can see this chap means business.

'Password! Who are you?'

'I'm an Argyll, four platoon. Put that bloody gun down, chum, it might go off!'

'Explain yourself. What are you doing here?' demands he, still keeping me covered.

'My platoon are on a working party. I was ordered to stay and direct another party. Two Engineers passed and said nothing to me. I've been waiting for a bigger party.'

'What is the password?' demands the runner.

'I never thought about the password; I thought I'd catch the others up.'

'What's the Colonel's name?'

'I don't know. . . .'

'Don't know!' The runner hastily interjects. 'What the b——hell d'you mean, you don't know?'

'Don't get the wind up, chum,' says I. 'I've only been up here a day, and I've not heard his name mentioned as yet.'

'You'd better come with me to my officer—and no b——monkeytricks, mind you, or I'll blow your b—— brains out. Get in front of me!'

I walk along the duckboards with a rifle and bayonet at my back until the front line is reached, where I am handed over to an officer who still doubts my story. I am put on sentry in the trench. As soon as I mount the fire-step, a shower of machine-gun bullets fly past my left ear, and my head unconsciously pops down for safety. I begin to wonder which is the better place—here, or over the top, wiring. I prefer to be in support—if this is a sample of sentry in the line—even if it does entail doing hazardous work at night, for I have no desire to act as target for a German gunner.

It is a very nice trench, firmly fixed and sandbagged, but for how long, no-one is able to predict: perhaps by this time tomorrow the whole lot will be battered down. Who knows?

My section come in at last, and I am thankful when I am safely restored to my friends, and hear, when it is too late, that the password is 'Polo.' I wonder what the next game will be: perhaps Nap or maybe Napoo.

I cannot get much sleep on our return from the working party. Rats attack. Swarms of them and my feet are freezing. Still awake I hear the corporal shouting 'Stand to!' At dawn the usual morning strafe, thousands of pounds flung away in a few minutes. But I am glad to welcome the day, for the nights are too long, long hours of suspense, especially if it is at all quiet. It is more pleasant during the daytime; I can see where the shells burst and the wounded receive attention more easily.

After 'Stand to' this morning we are entertained by 'Skinny,' a cheery fellow who in better times sold papers in Edinburgh. He is always telling jokes and making puns and to all outward appearances treats the war as a jolly holiday.

Charlie, the cook's assistant arrives and each man receives his ration of bacon.

'D'you call this a ration?' calls a fellow, and before anyone can reply we all duck—a whistling scream is heard as a 'wind jammer' approaches. Skinny finds his bacon in the mud and shouts, 'I'll swap anyone this big piece for a little bit.' but there are no offers.

Having had our feet massaged with whale oil to lessen the danger of trench feet, Chiswell, Smith and myself sit in the open writing letters and talking.

The sun is shining gloriously, and our conversation terminates as we watch an air fight. One of our Sopwith Camels has been over the enemy lines taking photographs, and they do not like it. Four German planes are attacking our little fellow, but he is nimble, dodging this way and that.

'Look at him spinning down: he's going to crash,' says Smith.

'No! He's righted—look! He's going to make a dive for it over our lines!' I exclaim.

'You watch the Hun planes turn their noses now our Archie* shells are bursting round them,' says Chiswell.

As the anti-aircraft shells burst about the German planes, they turn towards home as quickly as they can, and thus the thrilling air combat ends.

'Here comes dinner. Same old bully stew, I bet,' says Smith.

Charlie, the cook's mate, is calling us 'hungry wolves' as usual. 'I say, Charlie, there's mud in my dinner,' ventures one of the fellows.

'Get out, you mad baboon!' retorts Charlie in mock anger. 'Look at me—you never worry about the trouble I have in fetching the stuff for you. Mud! Cast your blinking optics at me if you want to see mud! Look, I'm covered in it! Had to duck a thousand times. And think yourselves damned lucky you have anything at all!'

It is a welcome relief to the monotony of the trenches to be able to spend a few moments in the company of Charlie, who with his mock grouses keeps us in fits of laughter. After dinner I go for a sleep, in preparation for the usual night ops. Perhaps it will be a raid, or wiring, or building up the front trench.

It is now getting dark; we are waiting to go on a working party and the conversation is about things in general. Skinny is talking about 'a land fit for heroes.'

'That's all bunkum,' says one of the men. 'D'you really think that the land will be fit for heroes.'

Another says it is a catch-phrase to keep the troops from

*'Archie'—an anti-aircraft gun.

chucking up the war. Skinny believes the country will be grateful and that the soldiers, sailors and airmen will never want. Has not Lloyd George promised as much? Still, there are others who have no faith in the promises of a politician.

The sergeant yells, 'Fall in the working party!'

We are at an undefended corner of the line, filling sandbags and building up the parapet. The stench is awful, like dead bodies—Fritz is active, and 'minnies' are rolling over and bursting with a terrible concussion. His machine-gunners are also very active, and it is risky work tonight, and a great deal has to be done. The enemy artillery has been effective in this quarter during the past twenty-four hours, and if we cannot repair this breach tonight, a wiring party will have to go out and strengthen the entanglements. If Fritz attacks here and our flanks fall back, things will be in a pretty mess. It is desperate work: reminds me of stopping up a breach in a dyke, working against time and the raging sea. It is hard work, too, and I frequently spit on my hands, as my skin feels shrunk. I will never make a good gardener.

I take a turn at building up, which is slow work, as Véry lights are continually shooting up making bright a wide area as they float down on their tiny parachutes. At last the job is completed and old Frère Boche has been kind.

I have finished writing letters for this morning. These are censored by the officer and collected by the ration party. Some of the men are playing cards, four others are singing a rude song. Another chap enquires if our gunners are firing short.

The corporal informs him that the German gunners almost surround us owing to this horse-shoe shaped line and that they command all the high ground.

Dinner is served. Same old bully stew flavoured with mud. Today we have a delicacy called 'Sandbag pudding': hard biscuits powdered and mixed into a pulp, a few sultanas sprinkled into the mess which is then boiled in a sandbag. What a hairy concoction, and sometimes a hungry man will chew away at a piece of cloth. One must see the thing before it is cut up to realise how like a fat hairy caterpillar it is.

Making my way to the dug-out there comes a short piercing hiss followed by *Crump! thump! bang!* behind me. One of our chaps has been hit in the chest which we dress. He is put on a stretcher and taken to the dressing-station. 'This is a bloody war!' cries the sergeant.

It is. All those ships sunk by submarines or mines. The lives lost and the enormous cargo, particularly food, sent daily to the bottom of the sea.

Whizz! thud! bang! go three shells in rapid succession, and we scatter as Skinny yells, 'We plough the fields and scatter!'

Another day is over and another night is drawing nigh, but I have not eyes for the pageant of the evening skies, for I am detailed for a wiring party. As we creep over the top, I try to analyse my feelings, and can only think of the picture by Bruce Bainsfather called *The Lovely Moon* which sums up my sensations. The top half of the picture depicts a damsel at home looking out of her window and saying to herself 'What a lovely moon! And to think the same old moon is shining on him!' The bottom half shows a wiring party, the same old moon, and Bill saying, 'This blasted moon is going to be the death of us!'

I shall probably laugh at my fears as I think of the incident later, for it is a good thing to be able to look back upon some of these nightmares and be amused at the scares. Tonight we get the wiring done in double quick time, and return safely to our dugouts to rest and maybe to sleep, for those who are fortunate enough not to worry about rats.

As usual, we stood prepared in the early morning for the attack which might come, and since breakfast I have amused myself by throwing pieces of earth on to the other fellows when they were not looking my way, each time a shell burst near. I have enjoyed watching the others duck while exclaiming 'By Jove! That was a near one!' or 'My tin hat just saved me!' But this pastime is only a bit of camouflage, as my nerves are on edge. There is nothing more trying to the nerves than to stand in a trench doing nothing while the shells burst around. One cannot retaliate, so one must make the best of things, and pretend. The physical shock caused by the detonating of these high explosives makes everybody windy although the fellows laugh and joke and pretend to read or appear unconcerned. We react in various ways, but whether we like it or not we get the wind up, we cannot help ourselves: the strain is so great and man's physical being is unable to withstand the shock.

I have now been in the line seven days, which seems to me

more like seven years. I feel an old soldier, for it is surprising how time drags out here: a day appears as long as a year; a night longer than that. And to think this has been going on day and night since 1914!

I address one of the fellows. 'Nutter, I feel as if I shall wake up one of these days and find this is all a dream. It seems too unreal to be true.'

'It's real enough,' Nutter replies. 'D'you know, Haworth, I often wish I'd been born a girl. I hate being out here. The old men get us into this bloody mess, and leave us to fight it out. We have to hate and hate, and I'd never even seen a blooming Hun before I got here.'

Nutter hands me a photograph. 'A picture of my girl.'

'Very nice and looks sensible. Same age as you?'

'Just eighteen. One of the best,' he replies. 'If she only knew how much she means to me out here.'

It must be our lucky day today for the sergeant hands us a packet of Flag cigarettes and a further surprise when he distributes a packet of chewing gum to each of the platoon. Where the chewing gum came from nobody knows and one of the boys suggests it was a contribution from the readers of some newspaper. Whatever the origin, the presents were thankfully received.

The sergeant has just left when a burst of high explosives put an end to our discussion. We duck.

'By hell, that was a near one! I think I'll have forty winks before tea,' shouts Nutter.

'I wonder what's for tea tonight?' I enquire.

'Roast chicken, I suppose,' returns Nutter, as he walks in the direction of his dugout.

We are now ready to go out on a patrol and the sergeant informs us we must return in two hours, as the Engineers are going to launch a 'projectile gas attack.' I have heard about this method at the Gas School, but have not yet seen one operated; I am greatly interested to see what happens.

'How do they work it, sergeant?' enquires Nutter.

'The Engineers have fixed gas shells—about fifty or so—all along our front line; they are all connected up with an electric wire so that they can be set off together. When the circuit is made, they are fired off simultaneously with a terrific explosion, and old Fritz has a concentrated cloud of gas flung at him.'

We set out on the patrol and at length return to the trench

without anything out of the ordinary happening. As we tramp along the trench there is a thundering roar and a terrific flame shoots out along our line about a hundred yards away. We automatically stop, such is the shock.

'Looks as if Fritz has mined our front line,' I whisper, much perturbed.

'No, it isn't a mine,' answers the sergeant. 'It's the projectile attack. Old Jerry will be quiet now for a bit. Hurry along, boys, and let's get over the road while the going's good.'

I retire early for a sleep, having had no proper sleep for ten nights. I am awakened by the order 'Stand to' for I have slept the sleep of the just, undisturbed by rats or bombardment. There is a nip in the air this morning, and the sun is just coming up. The enemy is awake, too, and is pounding our lines to smithereens. He means business this morning—not the usual morning strafe. Above the roar of the bursting shells, the corporal yells, 'That b—— gas attack has caused this!'

The enemy are certainly getting a bit of their own back, and we are powerless to intervene.

'What's our artillery doing? Why don't they barge in and stop Jerry's guns?' shouts one man in alarm.

A runner comes down the front line, and shouts, 'The front line's been blown to blazes during the night, and Jerry's knocking hell out of the earthworks again. It's like hell let loose!'

'I heard no shelling during the night,' I venture to remark.

'You're b—— lucky you were able to sleep, then, or you'd have been scared stiff,' retorts the runner as he continues his way down the trench.

Fritz is now working himself to a standstill. It is now quiet. Does he mean to attack? I wonder.

'Perhaps the gunners feel like breakfast,' murmurs the corporal.

Our artillery now commence a heavy bombardment, and the shells rain thick and heavy upon the enemy lines, thereby showing them what we can do.

'From what I can see of things, corporal,' I say, 'it'll be quiet after this until the afternoon.'

'Yes. There's been a smell of real spite in the air this morning. I knew it would happen after that gas attack: it's always the same.'

We have finished breakfast, and things are fairly quiet this morning; there is an ominous feeling that something is going to happen this afternoon. Our platoon do not allow this to worry them, and we are taking advantage of the quiet and cleaning ourselves up a bit.

It is still quiet, and after dinner I go into my dugout for a nap. *Sheeze! Whizz! Thump! Sheeze! Whizz! Thump!* go two shells in rapid succession, followed by the clanging of the gas alarm and the sounding of rattles. I hear someone shout 'Gas!' and I hastily put on my respirator.

A terrific bombardment commences and familiar scenes change like magic. The supports are now getting a sample of what the front line had earlier in the day, and I decide to stay in the dugout until things have quietened down. There is a possibility of being buried alive here, but it is by far the safest place while this scrap-iron is breaking up and flying about. My face is becoming hot, and the glasses of my respirator are steamy, but this discomfort is nothing compared with what might be if we had no such things as gas-masks. They have saved many a man from an agonising death, and no wonder we call them our best pals. The danger is over, for I can hear some of the men singing one of our favourite songs, so I go out to join them, for I love a sing-song.

It is now getting dark, and the sergeant is picking 'volunteers' for wiring. 'You, you and you,' says the sergeant, as he selects the men he desires to accompany him on his nocturnal expedition. I am not sorry when we come in again and return to our sheltered dugout once more.

This morning we are discussing schemes of how the war should be carried on. Nutter has suggested that Kaiser Bill and Lloyd should stand in a trench and fight the matter out between themselves. We agree it is a sound scheme but not practicable, and Nutter's motion is lost by six votes to two.

'What about a song?' cries MacDonnell, who is not in the least interested in the discussion, and he immediately pitches the mournful tune of one of our favourite songs of mock funk. We all join in singing:

> I want to go home, I want to go home,
> I don't want to see the trenches no more,
> Where the Allemandes drop whizz-bangs galore,
> Take me over the sea, where the enemy can't snipe at me.
> Oh my! . . . I don't want to die,
> I want to go home.

Adventure

Bang! Wallop! Thud! Crash! For the past fifteen minutes the earth has been powdered into dust which rises skywards intermingled with the acrid smoke released from the HE shells. The smoke is gradually dispersing and the poisonous fumes are being wafted upward into space. The air is becoming clearer, and breathing is more comfortable as the unpleasant and injurious odours disappear into the clouds beyond. It has been an ordinary everyday strafe, which like a mighty earthquake has shaken the very foundations of our small world.

The worst is over, and Skinny emerges from a funk-hole with a broad grin upon his round face. He looks upon this unfriendly shower of German shells as a joke—or pretends to. It is a waste of mental energy to think otherwise, and as no personal damage has been sustained, we can afford to laugh. Skinny amuses us with tales of imaginary persons attempting to 'swing the lead', as he calls it—swinging the lead being a term applied to men who attempt to evade duty by declaring their unfitness for service.

'The MO's are up to all the tricks of the trade,' says Skinny with a smile. 'It was said that if you swallowed a piece of soap it would make your heart wobbly. Well, some fellows did this just before the time appointed for a Medical Board, but the MO's got wise to it. One day a chap swallowed a bar of soap.... gradually, I mean—little bits at a time, not the whole bar at one gulp. The MO put this fellow into a hot bath and in no time bubbles the size of balloons oozed from every pore in his body.'

Above the roar of laughter, Skinny exclaims: 'They sent the poor blighter back to duty.'

The conversation now centres upon the subject of self-inflicted wounds, and the corporal is saying 'It's an extremely rare occurrence. In fact it's futile to attempt it, for the odds are all in favour of being found out, and that of course means punishment, apart from the possibility of grave injury.'

'How can it be found out?' enquires Nutter.

'Easy,' says the corporal. 'A bullet fired at close range makes an ugly wound which tells its own tale. Chaps are supposed to have tried firing through bully beef tins, or through sandbags, but the marks were always plainly visible: pieces of bully beef or tin, or a ring of sand round the wound. Secondly, it's not a difficult matter to tell the difference between a wound caused by a German bullet and that caused by one of our own. No, chaps, it's not easy to get away with a self-inflicted wound, and consequently it's very seldom attempted, however much a fellow is fed up with this hell.'

'Personally,' says MacDonnell reflectively, 'it's not worth the candle, for it's easy enough to get a packet without inflicting it on oneself!'

'That's what I say,' interjects Nutter. 'There's a piece of scrap-iron, or a little spot of lead flying about somewhere or waiting to be fired, with our names and numbers written on—and all I hope is that mine is a little spot of lead which will do me no great harm.'

At last we are being relieved. It is dark and, except for machine gun fire, it is quiet as we hand over to the new troops. I experience a wonderful feeling which I am not able to define, and the formalities of handing over being completed in whispers, we leave, a section at a time. We soon reach Ypres and double quickly but quietly through the town.

We have marched for an hour from Ypres and now fall out for a rest. From this position the Véry lights can be seen encircling the Salient, but danger appears miles away, although at first we speak in whispers from force of habit, until someone starts singing *Annie Laurie*, and our tongues are loosened. After that we have *Loch Lomond*, then other songs are rendered.

We march on again and, after an hour or more, arrive at a small camp where we are to spend the night. I lie down to sleep on the floor of the Nissen hut, undisturbed by shelling or other forms of frightfulness, without dreams which can be described as such.

I awake as the sun is shining through the open door of the hut, and as other men are already astir, I get up and leave the hut in search of water for a wash; I find some, but not enough for a bath. We have a good breakfast, and the QM comes round making notes of deficiencies in kit, after which he pays out twenty-five francs each, but there is nothing here to spend the money on.

In the afternoon we move further down on a light railway to a village of the name of Winizeele, which is about fifteen miles from Ypres.

4

Winizeele

Ypres, for me, is romantic, and before I arrived in Flanders, that martyred city, shelled into ruins, held in my thoughts something very precious. When at the Base Camp at Etaples I was informed our destination was Ypres, I was thrilled and proud to know I was on my way to 'Wipers.' My baptism of fire was over. I had been fascinated by the great firework display which—nightly—almost encircled us, when time stood still, and hours felt like days, but I am glad relief has come, although I would not have missed the experience. Now I enjoy a short season of rest in this country hamlet, Winizeele, somewhere in the north of France. When not engaged in war-time activities, I was learning to estimate the approximate landing of a shell. The whizz-bangs however came with a whizz and a bang too close to feel happy. The 'coal-boats' flung pieces of earth into the air weighing over a hundredweight: not at all good for the nerves. But in our locality, when five had dropped, we could count on several hours before receiving a further ration. The Hun gunners craftily used to mix gas shells with their heavies. Gas-shells come with a 'flop' and can easily be mistaken for duds. During a lull, the more seasoned chaps retailed earlier battles and gruesome scenes when dead men had been blown out of their shallow graves.

Before coming out here I had listened to tales by returned soldiers who advised me to keep out of it if I could. But I could not get the feel of things as recounted by the narrators. We can teach history, geography, mathematics and the like, but we cannot teach experience. We must experience for ourselves, and this is frightening, for we cannot convey accurately our feelings and emotions throughout any given experience.

After nightly spells of patrols in No-man's-land to capture prisoners for interrogation, over the top fixing barbed wire, or building earthworks, we were left bewildered. As we filled the sandbags, the stench was almost unbearable, for in the darkness we knew the solid stuff was not wire or stumps of trees, but in all probability we were digging up graves.

Our minds reached a point—or at least mine did—when we could not tell whether time was real.

It seemed so unreal, and yet we lived in a world of unknown but real possibilities. The individual may be free, but we cannot in this world exist without the service of others.

This can be said of the regiment with its discipline. We hold fast together, subject to orders, yet free as regards our inner selves. Officers and NCO's fall, killed or wounded: it is then that the private soldier takes command. That is freedom and discipline.

When at the Base Camp at Etaples I borrowed a book, *The Student in Arms* by Donald Hankey, from the Church Army library. I was attracted by the title, as I considered myself to be a student in arms. I read page after page, fascinated. Alas, I had to return the book only half read, as we were moving forward. I pondered upon the ideas Donald Hankey had set in motion and I felt that somehow I knew him. He reminded me of my Scout hero, the Hon. Roland Phillips, writer of The *Patrol System* and *Letters to a Patrol Leader*. I met Roland at a Patrol Leaders' conference and he influenced my ideas. I was never to see him again, for he had been killed in action. His spirit lives on. And so with Donald Hankey, for on my first rest after being in the line, Donald comes back to me: in this old barn with a covering of unclean straw, I discover a copy of the book as I make a place in which to sleep.

Chalked on the outside walls of the barn are reminders of lads who have gone before—Royal Scots Fusiliers, the HLI. It seems a holy place where men weary in body and mind will continue to come to rest until this war is over. I have a feeling of how like the stable at Bethlehem it is. We see pictures of the crib, with the animals and the family of Jesus surrounded by beautifully clean straw. I would imagine that first stable to be covered with dirty straw like this: none the less, more comfortable than the trenches, a place where we can lay our heads.

Now for washing. I intended to wash my shirt, but the dirty slimy green water of the pond makes this operation impossible. Milk can be obtained from the one cow on the farm, but no free issue. Having purchased *du lait*, my section scout around the

Working party going out at night

A 9.2 railway gun about to open fire at nightfall

farm in the hope of locating chicken or other treasure which might be put to good use when darkness falls. We are like primitive man now, and if we are unable to purchase necessities, we 'scrounge' them, which to the mind of the serving soldier is quite legitimate as it often happens that money is worthless. On this farm, however, there is nothing to scrounge: troops have been here before, and Madame understands the psychology of the British soldier, and locks the cow up at night in case she strays. This is a wise precaution for if Madame left it in the field at night it would be cooked meat by the morning. When a fellow has not tasted meat since he left England, and is hungry—and we are always hungry—it becomes a natural instinct to kill the cow. That temptation is frustrated because quite rightly Madame desires to preserve her private property.

My thoughts continue to centre around Donald Hankey. Why should I choose his book at the Base Camp, out of the many? And what is more perplexing, why should I unearth a copy of the book in such a strange place?

The men dress up, feeling as gaudy as peacocks, and swagger to the village. Having lost Windwood, I chum up with John Fraser from Perth. He is nineteen years of age (last month), is of a jolly disposition, has clear blue eyes and the complexion of one familiar with the sun. We enter a house for a meal of *pommes de terre frites* and *oeufs frits*—a plate of chips and one egg—one franc. The dining room is dirty—we are repelled by the sight of big black gluttonous flies, a solid mass covering the plates which had been used by others.

'Hell!' exclaims Fraser. 'We can't eat here.'

'It's the best you will get in this godforsaken place, Jock,' says a man who is finishing a meal. 'All the other places are the same—covered with flies—they breed quicker here than lice on a soldier's shirt—and that's saying something!'

We do not like the idea but must feed, and having dined we get out quickly.

We take a walk on this glorious evening in late July. The warm breeze of the day gradually becoming cooler as the sun is sinking. Here is peace. What a different scene only a few miles to the east? We look for more to eat but no stores are available. We do come across a cinema run by the Army Service Corps, but that is full so we amble into the country. The men we meet are all friendly, no introduction being necessary for we all wear the King's uniform. We naturally came across a grumbler or two. One said he was in a 'rotten mob' but if we had said such a thing there would have been a tragic end to the friendship. Strange lads are British soldiers.

When men are thrown together, prejudice often breaks down and we come to know each other more easily. Would we be able to converse with every stranger we met in civilian life?

'If we could only take this extraordinary spirit of comradeship to Blighty, what a vast difference it would make to our country and the world at large,' says Fraser.

The cool breeze of a summer evening, the flight of the birds, the green and yellow of the fields, the scent of the hay and the delightful vision of trees adorned with leaves of variegated tints speak peace to our hearts. We rest on a mossy bank, and the silence is so intense that we make no attempt to speak for a while. The sun is setting, and the sky is darkening in shades of softest purple and burnished gold. Here is perfect peace, and, God be praised, trees yet unshattered by the hand of man. I break the silence.

'I'm supremely happy tonight, John. I feel as if I've reached a haven after years of turmoil. Living in the mud and desolation at Ypres has been a peculiar experience which for the moment I am at a loss to describe. In spite of the filth, ruin and death, I was happy, yet happy with a weight round my shoulders, and I suppose we're all happy to be here instead of leaving it to our children; and if we believe this is the war to end war, we must, if ever we do go home, instil into the hearts of those coming after us the true love of peace and the utter beastliness and futility of war.'

John hands me a cigarette, and after lighting up, speaks in a quiet voice.

'Yes, Chris, I think about it much the same as you, and I'm glad you look on things in that light. . . .

'Listen! Music! A banjo and singing! Come on, Chris.'

The singing of *Poor old Joe* reminds me of a Scout campfire at home. We find a camp of North West Africans who entertain us at their sing-song and we leave happy.

'What a wonderful evening,' remarked Fraser as beneath one blanket we go to sleep.

Once again another dawn, and I feel refreshed in mind

and body after a sleep undisturbed by rats, shelling, or stand-to.

This morning some go on fatigue duty, as 'rest' after all is not complete inactivity: all kinds of work have to be done, and some of the men have gone to a shell dump to spend four or five hours loading shells. My platoon go out into a field and play at war, which is more fatiguing than the real thing.

After dinner, Smith appears and pats me on the back saying: 'I'm leaving tomorrow—going in for a Commision.'

'I'm glad. A change from this hole. Best of luck, old chap.'

'Why don't you put in, Chris?'

'No thanks, I'm too young and inexperienced.'

'Nonsense. You'll be trained. Think it over.'

All this is new to me. I have to be tested under fire of a big attack, and until that, I could not say that I would qualify to lead men through a dangerous operation.

We 'fall in' and parade for a bath. A small hut by the side of a dirty-looking ditch. We wait on the roadside as the bath is not ready. An Engineer pumps green water from the ditch into his boiler. When the water is warm, twelve men at a time enter the hut and stand beneath a shower improvised from jam tins, with holes punched in the bottom to make a spray. Something like a contraption used in the Boer War. The water is turned on. For two minutes a stream of water trickles upon our bodies, giving time for us to create a good lather; then the water is turned off and we have sufficient soap on our towels to wash a couple of shirts. After the bath, a clean shirt—clean as far as washing goes and this starts all my troubles. Within half an hour, I am itchy.

'I'm at last in the fashion,' I say.

'What's the matter? Have you got fleas?' enquires one of the fellows.

'No, worse,' I answer.

'Never mind, perhaps we will go to a proper delousing station next time.'

Several are scattered about the region, but if a new shirt is not issued one is bound to be chatty again as the eggs are hatched out.

'Anyway, I shall be able to join the other fellows in the "candle hunts",' I say.

Before tea the post arrived bringing the wonderful letters from home, and parcels of dainties, and now a few of us are going out to a quiet corner of the pasture for a banquet. We number five—John Fraser, Alex MacDonnell, Dewer, Nutter and myself—and selecting a peaceful spot under the trees, for the day is warm, we gather pieces of wood and kindle a fire, placing our mess tins on the glowing flame. The water quickly comes to a boil and Alex MacDonnell opens a tin of *Café au Lait* he has purchased from the canteen, and proceeds to make coffee. We sit down in the meadow, and the parcels which Fraser, Dewer and Nutter have received from home are opened and the contents spread over a ground-sheet. All kinds of cake and soda scones, sardines, chocolate, and a home-made loaf of bread, are on the ground before us, and we feel like schoolboys at a Christmas party. We have no butter, as those at home are not able to obtain sufficient for their own use, but the sardines will make up for any lack of that commodity. In the fashion of the backwoodsmen we use the bread as plates, which adds to the enjoyment of the meal as we are able to finish up by eating our plates, a thing we are not allowed to do at home.

'It's a pity Corporal Edwards couldn't join us,' says Fraser.

'Perhaps we can save some of this for him,' answers Dewer as he picks up another scone.

'This is better than balancing a cup and a plate on your knee in the drawing-room,' laughs Fraser.

'I simply loathe that,' says Nutter. 'I always edge near to a table, and if I can't, well, I just put the plate on the floor, which is more sensible.'

'All the same, I'd endure any ordeal like that if I could take tea in a drawing-room,' remarks Dewer.

'Why, what's wrong with this?' I enquire.

'Nothing at all,' responds Dewer. 'I'm enjoying this, and the rest—what I mean is, instead of having to go into the line again, I could invite you all to tea at home, where we could meet pretty girls, and dance and sing and play tennis and all the other things we ought to be doing at our age instead of standing up to our necks in mud and filth shooting other people we've never seen.'

'Have another sardine, Andrew, and forget all about the war for a bit,' suggests Nutter.

After Fraser has related the events of his last holiday in the Highlands, and the others have dwelt upon reminiscences of life at home, the war being completely forgotten, we decide to take a

Winizeele

walk before turning in for the night. The evening is clear and golden, with not a breath of wind, and as we walk we talk of many things.

Eventually we return to our billet, feeling tired, but not a weariness from fatigue: rather the feeling one has after a full day in the country, when feet are in need of a rest but the mind is alert and tranquil.

We were up at seven this morning, and have spent part of the day doing fatigues and skirmishing; now I am going with the same party as last night to the village. Here we enter an estaminet, and find ourselves in a large room crowded with British soldiers, mostly RAMC and Royal Engineers, by whom we are received graciously.

'Where are you down from, Jock?' enquire some medical men, at the same time making room for us.

'*Vin blanc* is the only stuff here, but don't have too much: it's pretty putrid, and the beer's worse. It's water taken from the ditch outside, and that's a sewer, so leave it well alone, Jock,' advises another man.

From another room come the strains of *Take me back to dear old Blighty*, and the pianist is doing his best on the old piano which has been in constant use since 1914 without having been overhauled or tuned. It is nothing short of a miracle that a semblance of harmony is extracted from the tired and overworked strings.

'The British Tommy is a marvel at doing most extraordinary things,' says Dewer. 'There's nothing he's not capable of doing, from talking Chinese and French, to winning the war on his own, and *Madame Française* always says "*Oui*" when the troops inform her they speak "*très beens Français*".'

'That's so,' I reply. 'But one thing very few are able to do is to speak German, but in spite of that we're often able to converse with the prisoners in a language of our own.'

I find myself listening to the troubles of a man in the Trench Mortar Battery. One of their officers is 'a pig of a man' who has no sympathy with the men, cadges cigarettes from them, afterwards insulting them, saying, 'This cig isn't worth smoking: I'll put it in my pipe.' The officer is hated and despised by the men, but because we are urgently in need of officers, a man of that type is given a commission and commands brave boys of nineteen.

'Don't take much notice of that,' I say in an effort to take the fellow's mind away from his troubles for a time. 'I've had some of that, for we had an unpleasant officer in charge of our company at Kinmel Camp where I did my training in a special boys' battalion before being finally drafted to my present regiment. The training was stiff enough, without a so-called leader of the "swine" type. We boys of eighteen, having had breakfast at six o'clock, were on parade in "full marching order" at six-thirty each morning, and remained at drills and exercises, physical "jerks" and bayonet fighting, until twelve-thirty. At half-past-two, parade again under NCO's while the officers had their afternoon sleep, and at six in the evening we came in for tea. After the meal the captain had us on parade again at seven o'clock to show our entrenching tools one night, a pull-through another night, kit inspection, pay, or a parade with our toothbrush, and on each occasion he was disfiguring a God-given face with a sardonic smile.'

'A man like that wants shooting!' interjects my companion.

'No,' I continue. 'That's a death a brave man desires. The compensating balance to life at that place was found in the Church Army and Free Church Rest Huts and canteens: full of kindness, smiles and cheerful conversation from the lady helpers who took turns at staffing the canteens at night, and never failed to dress the tables with fresh flowers from their gardens.'

'You seem to find good points in army life, chum,' says the man.

We join in a bit of singing interspersed with snatches of conversation, and at length bid adieu to our friends and depart. We leave the village wending our way through hop-fields. The golden evening has given way to a silver-clear twilight, a sickle of moon adding charm to our ramble. We are in a joyous mood as each tells an amusing story of pre-army adventures taking our minds off the war.

Dewer relates an incident when he was working late with a senior clerk. He ascended a skylight to the roof of the office building which overlooked the town square and, hiding behind a chimney stack shouted, 'Murder! Murder! Murder!' In no time a home-going crowd assembled. The only light in the building was in the office where Dewer was, and as police banged on the door, he hastily retreated and told the Senior who was on his way to open the door. Dewer had to hide in a deed box where he remained until the police had searched the offices.

Winizeele

I awake this morning with a smile as I recall the amusing episodes of last night. Fraser is beside me and we engage in conversation.

'When you come to think of it, Chris, we do see life in a different way. I've been thinking of the things we are missing at home—our friends, courtships, games, promotion and decent conditions. When we get back we'll have to learn all over again, and in the meantime the other fellows will be taking our positions. We stand to lose everything we hold dear in the world, but it's worth it, for we are able to do something for the world at large, and forget ourselves for a bit.'

Skinny is up and dressed, and is wearing across his chest a row of cardboard medals; with mock ceremony he impersonates a General. He carries a stick and to the imaginary sergeant exclaims: 'Take that man's name, Sergeant! Fourteen days CB and no more service in the line for not being out of bed for the General's inspection.'

Coming to the next man, he roars with mock authority: 'You look tired, man! I'm frightfully sorry, old man, but don't worry: just stay in bed and rest. Sergeant! Will you please bring some breakfast to this weary fellow? Make it two eggs, will you, and don't forget plenty of toast.'

Our sergeant now appears in the doorway of the barn, and shouts: 'Come on, lads, time you were up!' and turning to Skinny, smiles, then says: 'Breakfast's ready, Skinny. Get another man, will you, and bring it from the cooker,' and Skinny divests himself of the decorations and reverts to an orderly man.

After breakfast Skinny comes to us and offers each a cigarette from a tin of fifty Woodbines. He is a most generous chap, and his generosity is often the result of his own spending, as unfortunately he has no relative at home to send him parcels. We see to it that he shares in all the parcels we receive, and in return we must accept his offerings, or he would look upon himself as a scrounger, and refuse to share in our treats. His face is beaming, and he delights in telling us that the Signals Officer has presented him with the cigarettes, a gesture which means more to us than the tin of cigarettes.

5

Gloria

> O Woman! in our hours of ease
> Uncertain, coy, and hard to please,
> And variable as the shade
> By the light quivering aspen made;
> When pain and anguish wring the brow,
> A ministering angel thou!
> *Sir Walter Scott*

At the end of four days' rest, we are now moving to the 'forward area.' It is Sunday, and we sit in trucks travelling along the light railway which winds its way through hop-fields. We sing all the favourite songs as we steam along, now leaving the hop-fields for lines of hutments accommodating Engineers and RAMC units on the lines of communication.

We go dead slow in some parts of the track, and are able to converse with the men on the line. Asking some men where we might be heading for, they inform us it might be Messines or anywhere. It is always the same on these excursions: we never know where we are going until we have arrived at our destination, which is annoying, as most people like to know where they are bound for, instead of being moved about like pawns.

It is dusk when we get off the train and complete the remainder of the journey on foot, each step bringing us nearer the front line. The order is passed down the column, 'No smoking, no singing' we are near our destination.

The trenches at last. We are relieving a 'Pal's Battalion', who have been shaken up a good deal and are desperately glad to be leaving. As we take over duties in the front line we listen to the reports of the departing troops. That morning they had been caught unawares, Fritz coming over on a raid. The preceding bombardment had been so intense, the heavy shells bursting on the parapet, that the few men holding the trench withdrew to the support trenches. Eventually the Machine Gun Corps on the right had beaten off the enemy.

When the raid started, three Engineers were working over the top, and were wounded. The raiders picked up one of the lesser wounded men and carried him off—the raid was undoubtedly for the purpose of taking a prisoner for interrogation, as the enemy are expecting us to attack. The other two wounded Engineers were also picked up, but instead of taking them to the German lines, they brought them and laid them down beside our front trench.

'A thundering sporty action! And to think we're going to knock hell out of those Germans tomorrow!' I say.

'Goodbye, Jock, and the best of luck!' whisper the tired men as they depart for a well-earned rest.

Two men are posted to keep sentry in our bay, and Fraser and I sit on the fire-step. It is not a very dark night: a summer night is never really black, and even when the sky is overcast, our eyes become accustomed to the darkness and we can see. Fraser, usually loquacious, has not spoken much during the day.

Something had disturbed him and, in time, he mentioned a letter he had received from his girl friend Gloria. Her father had been killed in action last week.

I expressed my sympathy and told him not to worry too much. All the same, I felt a momentary convulsion of hate towards the enemy. This I knew would not be lasting for it was the first reaction at the news, an expression of my feelings for those who had lost a loved one.

We are soon to make a big raid in order to straighten out the line at this point, no doubt as a prelude to a coming offensive.

In the grey dawn we are waiting in the trench for the signal to attack. At last the bombardment commences, and to the thunder of the guns and the lightning of the bursting shells, which makes my head feel as if it were splitting asunder, we leap over the parapet, and shout and roar above the storm of the barrage. Suddenly I encounter one of our men, who has lost his reason. He is hatless, his gas respirator missing, and has no rifle. He springs on the back of the Lewis gunner in front of me, and attempts to wrest the gun from him, shouting, 'Give it to me! I'm going to Berlin!' and for the sake of our own safety I am compelled to give him a stinging right under the jaw. We get to the enemy gunners who are putting up a splendid fight in order to cover the retirement of their men. Breaking through the gunners, we leap on again, when I find another man with his mind unbalanced, standing over a wounded German and demanding souvenirs at the point of the bayonet. The German boy is screaming, '*Merci! Merci!*' and I am forced to thrust my bayonet to the breast of one of my own countrymen and order him on; to my relief he goes on. I touch the wounded German's hand as I go forward, as a sign to the terrified creature that he will be safe, an action no doubt inspired by the bearing of Fraser under his bereavement. The fearful strain and the terrific bombardment has caused those men to lose their reason completely, and ultimately they will be sent down the line as mental cases.

I am not able to recollect how long it takes to get to our objective. It does not appear long, but it is impossible to account for time on these occasions. I only remembered firing ten rounds of ammunition, but as I count up, and my pouches are fastened, I find I have fired twenty-four rounds.

We must now consolidate and prepare for a possible counter-attack. Victory is ours, but at what a cost of useful human lives: old pals lost and wounded, and our platoon again much below strength. Dewer and Fraser are by my side, but Nutter is missing.

'What's happened to Nutter?' I enquire with much concern.

'He was hit in the side coming over,' answers Dewer.

'Very badly?'

'I don't know. I saw him fall, and he was in great pain. The stretcher-bearer will perhaps be able to let us know something.'

It is quiet during the day, and the recent action has apparently taken Fraser away from his sorrow. Out here we have to cultivate what may appear to be hardness of heart. We see so many good friends killed and smashed up that to dwell upon those happenings would reduce us to insanity. And so as one body after another is broken and battered by the powerful goddess of war, we try to think that God has a bigger job for them to do.

A heavy shelling goes on through the night from both sides, and the dawn is now breaking; with it comes a fevered anxiety, for we fear an attack. Fraser is melancholy again this morning, and turning to me, says, 'Christopher, will you do me a favour?'

'Certainly, old chap. What is it? You're not worrying, are you?'

'I can't understand myself. I feel something is going to happen.'

Gloria

'Nonsense, John, you're not feeling well, that's all.'

'You'll be all right when we go down for a rest,' interjects Dewer.

Fraser continues, 'I don't wish to burden you fellows—the best pals a chap can hope for—but I've had this feeling for two days now, and I want you, Christopher, and you, Andrew, if you'll do it, to write a letter to Gloria if I go west this trip.'

'Of course we will, John!' cries Dewer.

'Yes, of course,' I whisper, for I can see in his eyes that he will leave us. I have seen the same look before in the eyes of men who shortly afterwards have passed over to the other side. It is one of those mysteries we have not yet fathomed.

'Cheer up, John,' I say as I squeeze his hand. 'All will be well.'

The officer comes round with the rum ration, and informs us that an attack is expected as we man the posts.

A severe bombardment now opens and a barrage of high explosive shells detonate directly in front of the trench; the German gunners have apparently misjudged the line and no harm is done. As the fire increases, we stand firm, our jaws set tight, eyes resolute, and await the advancing hordes, for the enemy are coming over and are greater in number than we are.

We open fire—rapid rifle fire, Lewis guns, and bombs—holding the enemy in check twenty-five yards away. The din is awful and above the tumult of the bursting shells, machine-gun and rifle fire, is the yelling and shouting of the men and the piercing screams of those who have been hit. German stick-bombs fly over, and in return our Lewis guns play havoc, and the enemy casualties must be enormous. I take over a Lewis gun as the gunner is killed, and pour lead into the advancing hosts until a bullet sticks in the breach which stops the gun from firing, and the enemy attempt to dash through.

'Some b—— bombs, quick!' I yell. 'The gun's stuck.'

The supports are now running forward to fill up the gaps. We pick up the oval hand-grenades and fling them over like cricket balls, two boxes being used to good purpose, and now the Machine Gun Corps come to our support and enfilade the attackers who, finding resistance too strong, retire badly broken, leaving wounded and dead behind.

I am parched and feel as if I could drink a brewery dry. Water bottles are soon emptied, and the wounded are being attended to.

A lump comes into my throat as I find Fraser about to breathe his last. He is badly hit in the chest and shoulder, but still conscious, and in a broken whisper he enquires, 'Are—the others—safe?'

'They're all right, John,' I say, not knowing whether they are or not, and at the same time I attempt to put on a field-dressing which I know will have no effect.

'Water!' cries Fraser.

I moisten his lips and his forehead, and a stretcher-bearer halts in passing, looks quickly at Fraser and goes on.

'Come back!' I cry. 'Come back, and see to him!'

The stretcher-bearer does not heed and attends to another fellow.

'Tell m-moth-er! Glor——'

And with a sigh John Fraser falls dead in my arms.

'God!' I cry, and react by cursing God for permitting such things to happen. A horror of loneliness and blackness of despair overwhelms me.

I pull myself together and carefully extract Fraser's wallet containing his treasured letters and photographs. On looking up, Dewer is standing by my side, a tear in his eyes, and blood flowing from a slight wound on his knee.

'Poor old John!' he murmurs. 'I'm sure he's happy—look on his face!' and giving me a gentle pat on the shoulder, takes out his field-dressing, and after painting his wound with iodine, puts on a bandage.

All through the day the German artillery have bombarded the roads in the rear, and now during the night the shelling is kept up, making it impossible to go down for rations.

Another day dawns in which I see no beauty. We are desperately hungry, and the agonising thought of not knowing when rations will come up, adds to our distress. If we knew that a meal would be available, say, in two or three days' time, it would be something to look forward to, but as it is, the terrible uncertainty preys on our minds.

The same stretcher-bearer whom I had cursed yesterday when Fraser was dying, comes along the trench. He is a remarkably powerfully-built man, with light brown hair, and from under his shaggy eyebrows there gleams a pair of grey eyes; but his face is gentle, yet grave, for he has seen more men die than any other in

Gloria

the battalion. He is a friendly character, refined and courteous, and speaks slowly with a Highland accent which is pleasant to hear. He approaches me saying: 'I'm sorry, Haworth. There was nothing I could have done yesterday and I had to press on to a chap with a severed artery. . . .'

'I'm sorry for my outburst,' I said. 'John was a great pal.'

'That's all right, laddie. Keep a stout heart.'

Corporal Edwards comes up with two magazines saying: 'I have an old copy of the Battalion Mag, and a copy of the *Gem*.'

I take the schoolboy adventures and live for a time with Tom Merry and his companions in a wild adventure with a spy in the vicinity of St. Jim's.

In the afternoon, I remember Fraser's pocket-book. The top letter is smeared with blood and other letters and photographs likewise marked on the edges. I will write to his girl-friend later.

MacDonnell is asleep. He has been picking up enemy wounded during the night. Skinny comes along and we wait for some of his jokes.

'Big advance on the Western Front,' he cries. 'Thousands of Americans ready for action.'

'We'll soon start the big push now, eh?' says Dewer.

'It's already started down in the south. Kemmel will fall soon.' Skinny had been talking to the signallers.

Skinny amuses us with his yarns, then tells a true story of a visit to a 'delousing station'. When undressing, they noticed a number of smiling Chinese faces peering over the partition. The Highlanders had been taken for women, so they covered their nakedness as they walked across to the showers. All the uniforms went through a stove and the big fat lice were exterminated, but the stoving hatched out the thousands of eggs nestling in the pleats of the kilt. 'In less than half an hour,' he said, 'we carried more chats than ever.'

In several places the trench has been battered down and large gaps appear. Being an old German trench we had to build up with sandbags—no easy job under heavy shelling.

In the afternoon, we see a haversack floating in a shell hole at the back of the trench, and two men crawl through the gap to retrieve the haversack, which is found to be attached to the back of an English soldier; how long the body has been lying there we cannot tell. Nevertheless there may be an emergency tin of bully on the body—and a tin is extracted from the haversack. The men attempt to bring the body to the brink of the shell hole, but Fritz commences shelling again, and the body is left in its watery grave.

We have some 'Tommy cookers' with us, and decide to make tea. Shell hole water must be used, as all the water bottles are empty, but a drink we must have, even if it is risky. One or two tins of bully and a few hard biscuits have been found hidden away in kits, which together with the bully beef found on the dead man, provide us with a meal.

Towards evening the heavy guns come into action again, but the ration party are able to bring up a few biscuits and tins of bully beef. The night is long and dreary, and as I take my turn on sentry I feel the presence of Fraser somewhere near, appearing to tell me all is well.

At last morning comes; our gunners have taken off their shirts and are pounding the German lines to bits, thousands of shells going over on their terrible journey of destruction.

During the day the enemy artillery cannot get the range of our front line, although they try desperately hard. As his shells fall short, the men shout back to him what rotten shots they are, some shells causing much amusement as they fail to burst. Suddenly there is a loud piercing scream, and a heavy 'coal box' drops behind the trench, our laughing faces changing like magic as we drop down quickly to the bottom of the trench with the earth falling on to us.

'Phew!' exclaims one man as he cautiously pops his head up again. 'By hell, that was near!'

We do not laugh so much now at the 'rotten shots.' I am severely shaken, for with the detonating of the shell, the earth seemed to open up, scattering tons of clay in all directions. Part of the trench was falling in broken pieces on top of me; I felt scared and indeed said a prayer while waiting in dreadful anticipation of more earth and pieces of iron hitting me. It was like Vesuvius in eruption.

As the effect dies down, and one by one the men get up, we burst into laughter as we look upon the scared faces of each other, which is good for it helps to relieve the tension and the shock.

The corporal exclaims with a grin, 'That one evidently didn't have our names and numbers inscribed on its nose-cap!'

Gloria

I have by this time recovered from the shock of losing Fraser, and feel more normal again, for the boys have been particularly lively, which has been cheering. As the sun is sinking, this sector quietens down, and the good news is passed down the trench that a relief is expected tonight. I am glad to receive that welcome information. I turn to Dewer and remark, 'This has been a warm place, and the sooner we leave the better.'

'Seconded with acclamation! I don't want to take a season ticket to this sector,' he replies.

'Carried unanimously!' adds MacDonnell.

Out on rest I miss the companionship of John Fraser, and think of the last time when on leave as a rose-tinted interlude, full of beautiful things, and sunlight and pleasant memories. I have got over the shock of his death, appalling as it was, and realise that he has only passed on to a fuller life.

Dewer, MacDonnell and I are drafting a letter to Gloria, a letter which, we hope, will be a comfort to a troubled soul. We have her last blood-stained letter in front of us.

Having sent the letter, we leave the billet—which this time is a Nissen hut—for a stroll, and in our talks with other men learn much of what others are doing. The man at home, and in fact we out here, know little about war, for it is impossible to imagine all the factors that make up an army in the field. Troops have to be transported by road, rail and canal, and the necessary conveyances have to be propelled, repaired and renewed. Stores must be staffed and fully equipped down to motor fire engines. Records of men and material kept, bread baked, roads made and kept in repair—no light task—bridges built and rebuilt when they are blown up, telephones and telegraph systems maintained, prisoners interrogated, fed, housed and clothed, messages deciphered, and hundreds of other things—of much of which the serving soldier is unaware.

One service in particular stands out before the men, as they are often brought into close contact with it—the medical service. If it were not for the casualty clearing stations, the appalling hideousness of war would be so overwhelming that the morale of the troops would go to pot. Every man going over the top hopes for a 'nice blighty' and if there were no certainty of being picked up, things would be too awful to endure. The service is a wonderful piece of organisation. First are the regimental stretcher-bearers who render first aid and bring their charges down to the regimental aid post, on to the field dressing-station, on again through other stations each of which do a little more patching up and making the patient more comfortable, until finally, and within a space of four hours after a battle, the casualty arrives at the CCS which is a fully equipped hospital capable of retaining numbers of patients for a period. How near these hospitals are to the front line in order to receive the wounded four hours after a battle, you may imagine. From the hospital there is generally a train service to the base hospitals, but in the CCS no urgent cases can be postponed and the major operations performed in one of those hospitals in the twenty-four hours after one battle was equal to those performed in a large city hospital in five weeks.

When the nature of the country is taken into consideration, it can be realised how quickly the medical units must act, for before the war the land in Belgium and northern France in particular was under cultivation. The ground was heavily manured, and not chemically, all human waste going into the ground, with the result that the fighting troops are carrying on their clothing death-dealing microbes. The most beautiful 'blighty one'—perhaps a bullet through the fleshy part of a limb—has cost many a man his limb or his life through the CCS not getting a case in time.

Apart from the surgical side of these establishments, there is the clerical, which is just as important; when a man is hit, news must be sent to the relatives of his progress, for it is also necessary to keep up the morale of the people at home, and it is no light task working day and night in a hospital.

As is usual with anything British, there is humour to be found amidst these gruesome surroundings which resemble small villages built on a morass. Each place is given a name: 'Bandighem', 'Mendingehem', and so on, the spelling being imitation Flemish but the pronunciation truly British.

At the base hospitals the women play their part in the alleviation of suffering humanity, and some women are to be found much nearer the line driving ambulances. The nurses, WAAC's and our womenfolk in general are working hard, and keep up a bombardment of smiles in spite of aching hearts, a part which carries no glory, no medals and no newspaper praise. They are wonderful.

'We've found some very interesting acquaintances tonight,' remarks Dewer.

Gloria

'And have discovered the war is a bigger thing than it first appears,' says MacDonnell.

'Small wonder that almost every man, woman and child has been drawn into the maelstrom,' I add.

We now approach the camp and, feeling tired, enter the hut in order to make ready our beds. Some men are in the hut already, with shirts off; holding pieces of candle, they are ruthlessly exterminating as many of the grey-backed lice as happen to be in the path of the flame.

'Gawd!' exclaims one fellow. 'What a whopper!'

Another chap, who before he joined the army was the chief office boy and 'general manager' to an estate agent, says, 'I'll swap two little ones for a big one.'

And so the talk goes on, intermingled from time to time with the 'crack!' of a louse as it perishes in the candle flame.

'I wonder where these things come from?' enquires one chap.

'They're supposed to breed in the sandy earth,' his chum informs him.

'Well, I wish to hell they'd stay in the ground instead of playing hide-and-seek in my shirt!' retorts the other.

Whether they breed in the sand or not we are unable to tell: what we do know is that the eggs come to life quickly in spite of repeated flame attacks.

'Let's have a race,' one man suggests, at the same time drawing a circle on the floor of the hut.

Another man accepts the challenge, and two lice of almost equal size are put in the centre of the ring, and the one which steps over the mark first is the winner. A low sport one might call it, but it provides amusement and distraction from the bigger troubles, and if we pretend we do not care about these worries, it helps us, for humour enables us to surmount many obstacles which otherwise would prove a severe trial.

The next afternoon finds us talking about religion, and 'Sandy Mac', a lad who came up with the last draft, is voicing his disapproval of the clergy.

'I don't approve of this "parson stuff",' he says. 'Wasn't it the chief priests and the scribes who planned and plotted to crucify Jesus? Aren't their descendants doing the same thing today? How about those who profess to be devout Christians—disapproving of this and that, laying down principles of life and conduct, and all the time—the dirty hypocrites—they are only going to church to save their own souls? I can't stick that kind of thing. That's why I keep away from church.'

'It may be as you say,' I add. 'But don't condemn them too harshly.'

'Aren't they for ever saying others are damned?' retorts Sandy.

'Perhaps so,' says Dewer. 'But is that any reason why we should?'

'I see Sandy's point,' I remark. 'We all desire God, I suppose, but it's easy to desire Him solely for His gifts.'

'We're wandering from parsons to church-goers in general,' says the stretcher-bearer who has been silent so far. 'Parsons, after all, are only human, and the conduct of the people counts equally as much as that of the priest; many so-called Christians expect their parsons to live a life far above that of their flock. They expect them to have wings, but as for themselves, a second-best will do. Yet God makes no distinction, and expects each one of us to use our talents in His service irrespective of merit or reward. I think it's Thomas à Kempis who writes, "Jesus hath many lovers of His kingdom of heaven, but very few bearers of His cross". Those who love Christ for His own sake,' continues the stretcher-bearer, 'will praise Him and bless Him even when things go wrong—believe in God, in joy or pain.'

'But isn't that being sentimental?' enquires Sandy.

'No!' answers the stretcher-bearer. 'God has no time for sentimentality. Sentimental prayer is no use either to God or man.'

The mail arrives, and we come down to earth again, as each man goes to his own corner to read the precious epistles from loved ones and to live for a time in the happenings of the sender. Occasionally a smile will brighten a face as the reader scans a passage about the cat being left in all night and eating up the week's ration of meat, or 'Mrs Jones wants you to look out for her Bert who is somewhere in France'—somewhere among the millions of British troops.

6

The Parson and his Parish

We have been in the line for short periods, where nothing unusual has happened, only the spate of death flowing on, flooding the trenches and the roads with blood, so that those who hereafter sup the wine of France will truly drink their blood and those who adorn their homes and churches with flowers from the French gardens in the springtime will know that their blood has enriched the soil which nurtured the fragrant blooms.

Kemmel has been taken by the Americans and all along the line the enemy is being attacked with vigour; soon it will be our turn to enter the fray.

It is September, and we are in a battered old trench at Voormezele. The sky is overcast and a light mist is rising. To the right of our position is Kemmel Hill, and directly in front is a German observation balloon floating in the air. On the parapet of the trench is a wooden cross marking the grave of a soldier, and beyond this, but which cannot be observed from the trench, is a wilderness of huge shell craters with what was formerly the towns of St Eloi and Zillebeke in the distance; further still is the ridge.

Here the battalion have come to take bearings, as soon the final assault is to be made by our armies. It is about five o'clock in the afternoon, and it is exceptionally quiet; Corporal Edwards and myself have been talking about the things we are going to do when the war is over. The sergeant, MacDonnell, Dewer, the corporal and myself are all that are left of the original platoon when I first joined it, and the reinforcements are new fellows just nineteen years of age, and a few not quite that; we more experienced men feel the responsibility of looking after the raw material and of teaching them life-saving tactics.

I am looking through the periscope and conversing with the corporal when we are interrupted by a whistling screech followed by a violent upheaval as a shell detonates, causing tons of earth to break up and scatter in all directions.

'Phew! that was a near one!' I exclaim as we both look round to see the result of the explosion, when *Thump! Crump!* followed by another mighty earthquake calls us to action, as the next traverse has been blown to bits.

'Shovels! Quick!' orders the corporal. 'A section's buried.'

We commence digging in deadly earnest, when scrambling over the top of the debris comes a fellow from the section we thought might be buried, and feelings are relieved as we ascertain the other men are safe.

'We'd better clean up before we're disturbed again,' suggests the corporal, and one of the section brings water from a shell hole in the rear in a canvas bucket provided for that purpose. We take a serious interest in our ablutions and even clean the mud off our boots, for although we have nowhere in particular to go, and it is certain that in a short time we will be covered in mud again, it is refreshing to feel clean in such a place, if only for a little while.

'Keep out of sight of that sausage balloon,' warns the corporal, which is just as well for the German observer is able to look down into our trench at certain points.

We begin discussing OB's and Germans in general, when we hear the sound of someone stumbling over the debris where the traverse had been. It is a padre, rather stoutly built, with a big round face displaying a boyish smile.

'Hello, boys!' says he, cheerfully. 'Things are very quiet in this district. D'you know, I've walked all along the road and I haven't seen a soul. I heard three shells burst: did you notice them?'

'I should jolly well think we did!' exclaims the corporal. 'One blew that traverse to blazes,' he continues, pointing to the heap of earth blocking the trench.

'Was anybody hurt?' the padre anxiously enquires.

On being informed there are no casualties, his face lights up again and he resumes, 'Well, when I saw those three shells, I had an idea that I was getting near to the line, so seeing an opening off the road, I turned in. I was rather surprised to find you fellows. In fact I am looking for the front line: the Wiltshires are holding the line not far from here. Is it much further?'

We burst into laughter. 'Well, sir,' answers the corporal,

pointing with his hand to the German observation balloon, 'do you see that sausage up there? Some blokes in the little basket must have seen you coming along the road, and no doubt those shells were meant for you.'

'Dear, dear!' exclaims the padre, 'fancy them going to all that trouble and expense to get a harmless fellow like me,' at the same time smiling at us and tapping his belt as a sign that he is unarmed: the only warlike equipment he carries is a shrapnel helmet and a gas respirator.

As we laugh loudly, the corporal adds, 'And this is the front line, sir; if you had continued your walk along that road you'd have found Jerry instead of the Wilts.'

'Bless my soul!' says the padre. 'How fortunate I was to meet you.'

'You see,' the corporal informs him with a confidence that would suggest he had known the padre all his life, 'old Fritz is continually shelling that corner, so we can't man that part of the trench. And, of course, the Hun gunners won't permit us to put up a notice indicating the front trench. The Wilts are on the other side of the road, sir.'

'Thanks very much. I must be going over to them now. Cheerio, you fellows, and God bless you!'

'Cheerio, and all the best!' we chorus.

The shades of night are now falling, and the sentries are posted in the trench, and the world appears to be standing still—not a breath of wind, nor the sound of gunfire—as if time had paused in its stride and is giving a few unconsidered moments of grace, the corporal resumes his chat.

'That C-of-E padre reminds me of another parson down at "Pop". He's in charge of a house called "Everyman's Club" in the Rue de l'Hopital. A quaint fellow, up to all kinds of tricks and dodges. He has a blind eye like Nelson and gets officers and men talking on all kinds of topics. The place itself is homely, and many of the men have brought gifts of furniture and other things to the house. At the back is a lovely garden containing one shell hole, and at the top of the house is a chapel—but I've never got as far as that, as I found the club the day before we left for the line a year ago, and I've not been there since.'

'How splendid!' I exclaim. 'I'd like to visit the place.'

'What's the name of the parson?' enquires Dewer.

'He is C-of-E,' answers the corporal. 'Clayton is his name, and after Communion in the upper room he takes it to the units in the forward area—the battery lines and balloon sections and others—sometimes getting as far as the front trench itself. He carries the sacred elements in a little—er—casket. . . .'

'Pyx,' I interject.

'Yes, that's it.'

'Why is it called "Everyman's Club"?' Dewer asks.

'Well, it's really called Talbot House after a lieutenant of that name who was killed at Hooge in 1915 in the first German liquid fire attack, and "Everyman's Club" because officers and men are made equally welcome.'

'We must make a point of seeing the place if we come out on leave anywhere near Poperinghe,' I add, my imagination being stirred.

Dick Blair, a new fellow, notorious for his filthy and blasphemous language, who jeers at the mention of the name of God or the church, has been listening quietly to the dissertation, and exclaims, 'It's all —— bunkum!' using an adjective which causes even a trooper to shudder. 'What has the church or bleeding parsons done in this world except make wars and cadge money from starving people to build churches and to keep themselves in luxury?'

'Don't be a damned fool!' cries the corporal indignantly, for he has met a number of parsons out here who by their sheer pluck and understanding of men have won from him the highest admiration. Although a stranger who heard him when under the stress of shell fire, or directing his team in action with a shower of curses, would judge him to be an atheist, yet in the quietness of the line he has actually encouraged religious discussion with those who would talk on the subject. He continues in the animated manner which is characteristic of him when giving orders of vital urgency, 'Don't the parsons come into this hell of a danger zone of their own accord? Would you come up here on a visit if you weren't obliged to? I'm certain I wouldn't!'

'What about our sky pilot?' thunders Blair in scorn. 'He doesn't trust his God to keep him out of danger, and you won't find him in the line.'

This is quite true, for our padre has never been seen wearing a tin hat, which gives an idea that he is somewhere out of reach of exploding shells. It is just as well that he does keep away from us, for he cannot bring spiritual consolation to men living in hell. They simply would not listen to him. He would find an extraordinary number of Blairs if he came hymn-singing and praying for our souls, which is what he thinks he ought to be doing. Our padre is too much of a spiritual being, and understands too little of this world and the affairs of men to do any good out here. The best that a priest can do out here is to be jovial and cheer the men by light conversation, take an interest in their work, and not be alarmed or distressed or discouraged by the blasphemies he hears, knowing that men are going through the biggest hell the world has ever experienced, and that they are white beneath. Under the stress and strain of this hell, men are fighting desperately to keep sane. A priest cannot talk solemnly of the goodness of God when shells are blowing human beings to atoms. There is no getting away from the fact that man feels hopeless in such a position. God will not stop this madness. God will not get comforts and food. What is the use of God at all? He does not help men in their despair. It requires a very strong faith to reason otherwise. The real priest will choose the right moment to talk of God, and—God be praised—many of them know when they ought to joke and when to pray.

As no-one answers the scathing remark made by Blair about our padre, he makes another rejoinder. 'If your Christianity is the only thing worth while, ask your Christ to stop this war, then!'

The reply which comes to my mind is, 'Will God interfere with the working of His universe in order to make a person believe? If we were to ask Him to blow us to smithereens and our souls to "kingdom come" we would be more certain of that happening.'

What I actually say is, 'MacDonnell has said already that this is man's own mess. Had we consulted God first, the war would never have started. As it is, we can't expect God to come in and stop it to suit our convenience.'

It is a wonder to me that men talk so much about God, when apparently the only thing He can offer them is death. The simple faith of most men out here is amazing, in a world which knows so much cruelty and misery.

A 'five-nine' crumps at the back of the trench, and we come down to earth where we remain until the air has cleared. Our conversation now resumes an earthly character. We yarn and joke and talk of trivial matters, and as darkness is upon us we stifle our laughter in case the enemy should hear us and come to the conclusion that we are too happy to be left undisturbed.

The sergeant appears, which brings our conversation to an end, for he orders the corporal to take out a gun team to an outpost between the German lines and our front line trench. In a whisper he details his instructions and the corporal, who is almost inaudible, selects Dewer, one of the new fellows and myself to accompany him to the 'sump hole.'

Jumping over the parapet we crouch after the corporal, who leads us to the small hole which has been scraped out thirty yards in front of our trench.

The new man is more windy than he ought to be as a first-timer, and perhaps this little picnic will do him good. We settle down, with hardly sufficient earth to conceal us, when the enemy artillery open fire and shower a barrage of shells to the left and, fortunately for us, they continue to creep left, otherwise our bodies would be mingling with the smoke and bits of earth.

As each shell detonates, the corporal pops his head up, saying, 'Keep your eyes skinned in case Jerry comes over'—for we are responsible for the lives in the front trench. A shell bursts behind us like the roar of machinery tumbling from the top floor of a mill on fire, making the earth quake, then bursting into flames which crackle and illuminate a wide area.

'Keep your heads down!' roars the corporal, 'it 'sa petrol shell!'

More shells follow, and find their mark behind our lines, and after a while we hear the thunder of violent explosions behind the lines.

'They've hit a shell dump!' exclaims the corporal.

Thunder! Rumble! Thunder!

'It'll go on exploding all through the night and perhaps all day tomorrow,' shouts the corporal above the deafening roar of the gun fire.

The new boy is so scared that he keeps his head down all the time, and it is apparent that we older men will be compelled to take all the strain and leave nothing to the youngster.

We continue our watch from the sump hole during the next day, being constantly on the alert for the sight or sound of the enemy who may come prowling round; shortly after dusk we come in and are glad to know another platoon will take on the job tonight, for we are as windy as the new fellow, but have the power to put up a good show and not give way to our fears. We are sorry for the poor youngster, who ought never to have been sent out; in fact he is only a few months younger than Dewer and myself, but we consider ourselves old soldiers now.

Having had a rest, it is early morning as we take up our turn at trench duty. It is much quieter than last night, the shelling not so heavy, although the Machine Gun Corps on the right are continually sweeping the enemy front with their fire. Suddenly a bombardment commences on our right, which appears to be somewhere in the Armentieres sector. The sergeant comes along the trench and says, 'Stand steady boys, there's nothing to fear; our artillery is going to open out with all the concealed batteries to keep old Fritz busy up here while our troops attack down south.'

The men who relieved us at the outpost come in, and smile as they drop in the trench. The sergeant leaves to warn the other men. We now hear the *crack bang* of our guns, then the *wobble* of the shells as they speed onward through the air, then the dull explosions as the heavy missiles shatter in a thousand pieces in the enemy domain, dealing death and destruction in their wake. The enemy machine-gunners, expecting an attack, are sweeping our front with bullets. Still the thunder of our big guns goes on smashing up the enemy gun positions.

'Old Jerry must be in a hell of a panic now!' cries the corporal.

The buzz of our planes can now be heard as they circle round the enemy lines, adding to the consternation of the enemy, who are unable to determine what is going to happen.

After an hour of continuous bombardment, our artillery cease fire, and quiet reigns supreme once more; the enemy guns have been silenced and do not reply. It is now daylight, and an officer brings round the rum issue. When it comes my turn, I cough, and smiling at the officer, say, 'I have a slight touch of the cold, sir.'

The officer laughs amiably and answers, 'I've heard that story before, and you can't have an extra ration this morning.' Then after a pause he continues, 'I feel damned sorry for you boys with no proper dugouts, but we should be leaving tomorrow'.

As the officer walks round the traverse into the next bay, Dewer and I have a chat, as it is quiet and we have nothing in particular to do at the moment.

'I can't understand young Blair,' says Dewer thoughtfully. 'His talk is revolting. I can understand a man giving vent to his feelings—we all do that—but that boy has no variety of expression whatever. He's simply odious, and I'm beginning to hate him.'

'We're not saints as far as swearing is concerned,' I say.

'I don't mind an ordinary curse now and again. It's sex and religion being treated in a filthy and blasphemous way which I detest.'

'The two main reasons why a young fellow swears are to relieve his feelings, and because he thinks it makes him look big,' I say. 'In his case I think it's for relief. It is a problem; but you will observe that the words dealing with sex and religion are the main topics. Why? Is it not because frank conversation upon those matters has been forbidden to him when a boy? Perhaps his first thoughts about religion were hushed up in such a manner that he became frightened, causing him to desist from further speech on the subject. His natural interest in sex had likewise been tabooed, but although he has not spoken freely about the subjects, having suppressed the thoughts as something very wrong, this interest, being natural, cannot die, and the boy finds relief in swearing. We must teach him that his interest in these matters is right and proper and not necessarily filthy.'

'I understand what you mean, Chris. We're in a similar position, I suppose, although perhaps not so acute. When we're penned up like rabbits and unable to resort to action under shell fire, we use swearing as a relief, and looking at the problem in the light of your remarks, perhaps the reason we hear the word "bloody" so often is because blood has made such an intensely vivid impression on our minds.'

'I can't say,' I observe, as I prepare to clean and oil my rifle.

'D'you think, Chris, that we have any hope of doing anything for Blair?'

'Of course. He's not altogether bad. All he requires is a little sympathy and patience,' I answer.

'I wonder if the stretcher-bearer could have a chat with him some time?' says Dewer.

'Yes, he's evidently the right man, but we can help if we interest Blair in our conversations.'

The corporal joins us, and in a matter-of-fact sort of way observes, 'We've just had a heated dissertation in the next bay on the efficacy of prayer,' and looking up at me, continues, 'D'you believe in prayer, Haworth?'

'Yes, I'm constantly pondering over the subject of prayer.'

'And what is your conclusion?' asks the corporal.

'I believe that in prayer we're able to soar above the confused tangle of doubts and perplexities of this life, and draw upon the inexhaustible resources of the infinite. I find myself praying at odd moments, sometimes in the quiet, sometimes under shell fire, sometimes even when working the Lewis gun.'

'What do you find to say?' enquires the corporal.

'For the most part I use no words at all. I place myself in the presence of Christ and contemplate on one of His virtues in quite a general sort of way. I don't attempt to argue or draw out all its implications. . . .'

'I must confess that I broke off the habit in peace time,' says Dewer. 'Now I'm up against it, I can't ask God to step in and save my skin now.'

'I believe that's the attitude of a great many men out here,' says the corporal. 'They don't care to ask for favours, but they must have something to hang on to, and inwardly they're hanging on to God, though they don't realise it.'

The sergeant comes up and we talk of things in general for a time, and attempt to instruct the 'windy' youngster in trench habits, but it is not much use, for on looking into his eyes, we perceive a terrified gleam similar to that of a small animal face to face with a deadly snake, petrified and waiting for the monstrous creature to consume him.

Crump! Thump! goes a shell, and bursts in the rear. The corporal fingers his respirator, expecting a gas shell, and then, looking up at the youngster, discovers he is not wearing his gas respirator on his chest. 'Where's your respirator?' he yells.

The boy is bewildered, and replies, 'I think I left it in the sump hole.'

'Here's a pretty kettle of fish!' exclaims the sergeant. 'What will you do without a respirator? If the staff find this out, they'll think you left it purposely in order to get gassed. . . . Whatever made you take it off? You always keep your respirator tied round your body in the line.'

It is dangerous for anyone to show themselves outside the trench during the hours of daylight, as hundreds of eyes are watching and waiting for the slightest sign of life or movement: waiting and watching, with machine guns and trench mortars and artillery, yes, and snipers disguised in the ruins of a shattered building, all ready to pour lead or shells into the body of one who might be bold enough to violate the sanctity of No-man's-land. But the corporal acts quickly. He springs over the parapet and cautiously makes his way to the sump hole to recover the respirator.

After an interminable time, in which I am filled with apprehension for his safety, he at length reappears with the retrieved gas mask in his hand, unseen by the enemy. Tumbling into the trench, he hands the respirator to the boy, saying, 'Here you are, lad. Tie it round your chest, and keep it there while you're up here. Consider yourself lucky Jerry has sent no gas shells over this morning, or you would know about it.'

I am unable to decide whether the boy understands the noble action just performed by the corporal, who without a thought of the consequences rushed forward on an errand of brotherly love, scorning the danger of being riddled with machine-gun bullets or torn asunder by shells which are relentless in their method of destruction. I cannot dig into the depths of the boy's mind, and unless he chooses to tell, will never know his feelings. On the surface there was no sign of gratitude or remorse as he took the respirator from the corporal; perhaps he feels more deeply than he is able to express either by words or action.

The sergeant looks at the corporal and myself, and his eyes flash out a message that the young lad must be kept behind the lines in future. Turning to the boy, he remarks, 'Lad, I don't think you look well. You'd better report sick when we arrive at our rest camp.' Now turning to the corporal, he says, 'See that he reports sick when we go down,' and lowering his voice so that his words are not audible to the boy, adds, 'I must have a talk with the MO about him, and fix things up.'

The day passes without any untoward incident, and the westering sun, now sinking behind a cloud, now breaking forth again shedding the last rays of golden light upon the desolate landscape, warns us that we must make ready for the long and lonely vigil of another night with the horrible monster of death and destruction lurking in the shadows.

As twilight turns to dusk, the sergeant details a party of men to go down for rations. Dewer is included, but I am left for trench duty. They leave our bay, to plough their way down the battered old trench to the road, where about a mile further back they will find the ration limber waiting to be unloaded.

I stand on the fire-step. The road is being heavily shelled as if the enemy are aware of the advent of our food-carriers. The volume of shelling increases, most of which is concentrated on the road, and I fear for the safety of our men. I have a feeling that all is not well with them. Here in the trench, in comparative safety, I stand gazing into the dark blue and grey shadows, which are constantly being illumined by the vivid whitish green light of the Véry lights shot up by the enemy. As each light soars into the air, bursting into a bright fascinating light, like rockets at the Crystal Palace for the amusement of the holiday-maker, and hovers above the shell-torn ground for several seconds, gently wafted by the slight breeze, my eyes scan the wretched wilderness of waterlogged shell holes and tangles of barbed wire, but I do not perceive anything in the nature of human life upon the dreary waste stretching before me.

At length the ration party return, carrying sandbags containing our food, and petrol tins filled with drinking water. The sergeant comes to me and in a voice which is almost a whisper informs me that Dewer has been hit by a piece of shrapnel, and sent down to the dressing-station. In the darkness it cannot be ascertained whether the wound is serious or otherwise.

'I think he'll be all right,' continues the sergeant. 'He was conscious, and seemed happy at the thought of going to blighty, so I don't think it serious, and he'll have immediate attention.'

Thus another friendship is broken, which in the passing of time I hope to renew, but for the present, I can only console myself with the thoughts that he is having a rest.

It is our fourth day in these trenches, and darkness is approaching. Word is brought to our section that the mess orderlies are among the casualties, and two men from the platoon are required for the job, as we are being relieved tonight. The corporal asks one of the new men, Robert Scott, and myself to take over the duties until arrangements can be made later. We are to leave the line before the battalion is relieved and I am glad, for it generally happens during a relief that the enemy think fit to pound the roads to smithereens, often resulting in more casualties than when holding the line. As it is now quiet, I have no desire to linger in this trench. Out on the road we are joined by the orderlies of the other platoons, each pair carrying a dixie on wooden supports, which rests on our shoulders similar to the arms of a stretcher. We stumble over the torn-up ground on our way to battalion headquarters, where the guiding officer is waiting for us. The enemy apparently has this position marked on his maps, for on our arrival at headquarters, shrapnel is falling like confetti at a wedding, but not as welcome, and we speedily scamper into a deep and roomy dugout. These are comfortable dugouts and shell proof, not as those in the trench which were built in Egypt's seven years of famine, or perhaps burrowed by rats, so small are they. These are made to withstand any amount of shelling, for have not the brains at headquarters to be specially cared for? Presently Fritz decides he has worked hard enough for a time, or perhaps the artillery gunners' union have objected to his working overtime without extra pay, a thing which happens on our side (only it makes no difference). We poke our little noses out of the dugout and sniff the air, and finding it healthy, we emerge into the open once more.

Shouldering our dixies, we march away to our billets, and as we accelerate our steps in order to leave the bursting shells behind, Scott and I find our load getting heavier. On and on we go, keeping double quick time, until we turn into a road flanked by battered camps lying desolate among the shell craters. Winnipeg Camp, Toronto Camp, Regina Camp had been used as rest camps when this district was more hospitable and the front line not so near to Ypres as it is now. On we run, with the weight of our burden cutting into our shoulders, and we wish all kinds of things for we are carrying more than a pack mule and are exhausted. We can keep up the pace no longer, and the officer calls a halt although he has no wish for an unpleasant encounter with fragments of enemy shells which are constantly hitting the road.

Off we go again after a brief rest, the dixie becoming more unbearable, for in addition to this, we are carrying full equipment. We pass through the remains of the village of Dickebusch, and after a march of miles and miles, or so it appears to us, we enter a small village which is to be our home for a few days. The officer directs us to our billet and then points out the position of the company cooker which is hiding in the shelter of a ruined house, and to the cook we take our burden. Pulling off our equipment and putting down our rifles, we say something about this being a 'hell of a war.' So fed up are we that Charlie, the cook's mate, looking at us in mock scrorn, says we ought to be at home cuddling a girl: that's all we're useful for, unable to carry an empty dixie a few kilos. We wish his words about cuddling a girl would come true; and now with a sudden start he exclaims, 'What the hell have you got here? I don't want this blasted stuff! This is a cookhouse, not Woolwich Arsenal!'

I look into the dixie and discover a box of Mark VII ammunition which someone, not wishing to carry the bullets themselves, had placed there when we were sheltering from the storm of flying shrapnel at battalion headquarters. Scott and I are indignant, and start a quarrel, asking each other why we had not the common sense to peer into the dixie when it became so heavy.

'Here, you hungry wolves,' cries Charlie, 'get some ber-goo down ye, and shut up!'

We shut up as we sample the ber-goo—porridge—and finding it good, praise the cook on his wonderful cooking, which is a sensible thing to do, for one never knows what a cook is able to do for one, especially if one bestows commendation on his culinary perfections—or imperfections as they sometimes are.

We leave the cook house to inspect our new billet and to await the arrival of our company from the line. The house was probably used as an estaminet, for the two front rooms, one on each side of a small hall, are commodious. The windows are shuttered with those quaint wooden doors peculiar to Belgium and France. This is to keep out the wind and the rain, not as they were originally intended, for now no glass remains in the window frames. The roof is missing, having been removed by a shell or many shells or perhaps bombs from a passing German plane, so that the upper floor is not in use. The part of the house behind the two rooms which will house our platoon is smashed up and it is impossible to get to the garden at the back owing to the piled-up mass of masonry and wooden beams. With the aid of a stump of candle, Scott and I endeavour to explore these ruins, for we are only boys and possess that inquisitive instinct to search for buried treasure. We are not able to discover hidden gold or any other form of treasure, but we do perceive the mangled remains of the household pump lying beneath the heap of wreckage. During our exploration we make use of several witty phrases, small wit indeed, and assisted by the generous helping of porridge which we have recently consumed, our heavy hearts have been lightened, and we are in a more jovial state of mind than when coming down the roads carrying a burden we would have dumped had we known what it was.

We conclude our investigations into the unknown corners of the house, and come to the front doorway, there being no door, as it has presumably been used a long time since by some British troops desiring warmth. Here we sit down for an interminable wait; the village is shrouded in darkness and seems a city of the dead, so intensely quiet it is after our period in the line; and then the reverberation of the guns can be heard and our company march into the ruined village, the tramp of many feet echoing through the still night. The sound is almost fantastic and ghostly; or is it the effect of the suddenness of my removal from the tumult of the shelling to the comparative quiet of this place preying on my nerves?

Scott and I feed the platoon on porridge and tea, and after naming our new home the 'Hotel Ouderdom', for this is the name of the village, we prepare for sleep. Our billet is facing the main road to Poperinghe and as I think of that town, the story of Talbot House as told by the corporal flashes before my mind, and as I dwell upon the impressions created by the telling of the yarn, I murmur to myself that there are places much worse than this, for here at least I can look forward with joyful anticipation to the morrow. Feeling comforted by my thoughts, I lie down to sleep beneath a lousy blanket, but who cares? I am tired and weary and could sleep on the edge of a precipice if necessary.

The Argylls crossing a railway, October 1918

The battlefield of Ypres in 1918

Troops on rest behind the line

7

Preparation

After a peaceful and refreshing sleep—despite the fourteen-mile naval gun in action from the railway line near by, causing the house to shake and loose bricks to fall from the upper storey each time it fires a shell—I sit up in bed, feeling how jolly it is to be alive. Scott and myself are still orderly-men and we must hurry along, as breakfast will be served shortly. After dressing, we leave the billet to look for water for washing. It is frosty this morning with a slight mist hanging over the village, which no doubt will disappear with the sun. We enter a ruined house in the hope of finding a pump. We do, but it is smashed up like the pump in our billet, so we retrace our steps.

We meet one of the cooks on the road and enquire from him if it is possible to find water, and he directs us to a ruined house where he says there is a pump still workable. The back portion of the house is almost impassable owing to the debris, but the pump is in its usual place, although reclining at an angle of forty-five degrees. We scramble over the heap of bricks and stones, and after a vigorous effort coax a trickle of muddy water, and thus we perform our ablutions.

Having carried breakfast from the cooker to the billet, we serve the platoon, and after the meal we relinquish our position to two other fellows whom the corporal has appointed orderlies.

The village, which in better times is a peaceful and quiet hamlet, shows signs of great activity this morning. Vehicle after vehicle is coming along the road from Poperinghe, British turning left, and the French right. A troop of French cavalry trots along, and I wonder what they are going to do. During the day we are kept fully occupied with various fatigues, and towards evening, battery after battery of artillery gallop up the road and turn the corner opposite our billet, almost on two wheels. Enemy planes are hovering overhead, presumably scouting, as they linger over the road but do not drop bombs, for which we are thankful. Now one of the biggest traction engines I have ever seen comes slowly puffing along, hauling a huge gun of the Royal Marine Artillery.

Tea has been served—the usual bread and jam—and Corporal Edwards, MacDonnell, Scott and I are preparing to go for a stroll to Poperinghe. The other fellows ask us to do a little shopping for them, and we have a string of orders for chocolate, cigarettes, biscuits and other commodities which we hope to purchase in 'Pop'; I am anxiously looking forward to visiting Talbot House which the corporal has spoken about. We have poshed up and some men in the billet ask if we are going square-pushing, which is rather remote, as we do not anticipate meeting any nice young girls in Poperinghe; in any case, any young lady found in that region will be busily engaged selling eggs and chips to the troops in the town; the few civilians who remain in such places do not abide there because they are healthy or safe places, but because of the harvest they will reap from the British soldiers. They (the soldiers) spend most of their money in these areas and some people have amassed large fortunes—and who can blame them for being so enterprising?

Making a final survey to see if our kilts hang properly, and gas respirators slung at the correct angle—for we are very particular about these small details, as the honour and prestige of the British Army depend upon them—we are ready to leave.

The sergeant enters the billet, wearing his battered shrapnel helmet, and turning to us, exclaims, 'Sorry, boys, but you can't leave billets tonight.'

'Blood and thunder!' yells MacDonnell. 'What's the matter now? Has Fritz broken through because we've left the line?'

'Nothing of the kind,' says the sergeant. 'You have to parade for "lice traps" and jerkins.'

A 'lice trap' is a woollen vest, so called because the cosy warm material attracts the chats. One or two grey-backed lice can be found in each little cell in the knitted garment, growing fat on the blood of the men. One fellow thinks jerkins is something to eat—tinned food in fifty-seven varieties, similar to pork and beans—and is annoyed and grumbles when he discovers he must carry a leather jacket on his back.

When this extra fatigue is finished, it is too late to take a walk

Preparation

to Poperinghe, and so we light candles and get beneath our one blanket in case further fatigues are required. I am tremendously disappointed at having been denied the visit to Poperinghe; but with the post several parcels have arrived for the platoon, and remaining beneath our blanket, we have a party, followed by a concert, each man giving a turn, a song or a yarn. One of the new boys has been in a church choir and has a particularly good voice.

Young Blair is continually interjecting vile remarks, and is admonished by the others. The stretcher-bearer is in the room with us, and speaks to the lad in his beautiful slow manner, but his voice is not much above a whisper, and his words are inaudible to me on the other side of the room.

Silence now reigns, as the men are dropping off to sleep one by one. When all the candles have been extinguished, and most of the fellows are sleeping, and just a few thinking, the boy Blair calls across to the corporal, asking if he is asleep. The corporal answers, and Blair says how sorry he is for having spoiled the spirit of the evening.

This morning has been so much hurry and bustle that we have had little time for anything but our preparation for the forthcoming offensive. The midday sun is shining with compassion upon the ruined village and the streams of men and horses who are passing along the road like ants. On many occasions when in the country I have watched the tactics of those fascinating insects: how they hurry from one nest to another, and never appear to become exhausted although carrying eggs as large as themselves. I have wondered at their orderly method when removing. One long unbroken line of the creatures carrying the eggs, and another line retiring empty-handed for a further burden, reminding one of the natives loading ships with coal in the east. But the ants are always in a hurry, and sometimes tumble over each other in their eagerness. One day as I watched them I thought how powerful I was, for with one movement which would cause me no exertion I could crush them with my foot and wipe the whole family out of existence. How like those ants are we, with the powerful goddess of war looking down; but like the ants, we have a sting, and in time we will overwhelm her and subdue her: that will be when we people, the ants of the world, have learned to love widely, and discovered the futility of war.

The remnants of the French cavalry come by: most of the horses are wounded, the war-weary animals led by a few French soldiers, and I wonder if the advance has already commenced and the enemy have left the trenches and pill-boxes.

We are ordered on parade again, and in double file we approach two dumps; one is a heap of pickaxes, the other a pile of shovels; as we pass we take one of these implements and fix it between our leather jerkins—which we are wearing over our tunics—and the straps of our equipment, one man helping another. Should we turn round suddenly, the head of the shovel or pickaxe rings against our shrapnel helmets. We are then issued with four Mills hand-grenades, and we place two of these in each side pocket of our tunics. Finally, extra ammunition is given to each man, and we are so weighted down that we can scarcely move. We are dismissed, and go back to the billet, where we unpack.

It is late in the afternoon, and the sergeant has gone to the officers' meeting for final instructions, and we pass the time away writing letters home.

The sergeant returns, looking upset, his usual cheerful countenance now extremely grave. Taking a piece of chalk he makes a sketch on the wall of the room, drawing the trench, which at zero hour will be the jumping-off place, and as he instructs, puts in dots here and there describing certain landmarks, now with a circle, showing the position of the 'craters near St Eloi we are to take.

The great battle is ready to begin. The General with his staff has devoted days, weeks and perhaps months of anxious thought to the planning of the operations. At zero hour the bombardment will begin; at such a moment the barrage will lift, and creep another fifty yards ahead, the attackers slowly walking behind the bursting shells. Two hours before the attack the concealed batteries will bombard the enemy positions. Instructions have been given down to the minutest details and at the last minute the carrier-pigeons will arrive which are to play their part with the runner, despatch-riders, telephone and telegram, to keep the General and staff informed.

It is time for moving, and the sergeant, much distressed and in a husky voice, wishes us the best of luck and shakes hands with each one of the platoon. My heart beats quicker than before, and as I look at the others I can see they are thinking. What are they thinking of? Death? No: they have looked him in the face;

Preparation

they have got accustomed to him and ceased to fear him. Are they thinking of loved ones? Yes: very tenderly; but the big thought is not only the appalling hideousness of war, but its utter futility.

The sergeant leaves the billet, and letters are collected—no doubt the last that some of us will send home. One or two groups of fellows are talking carelessly, but most of the boys are taking a last look at a treasured photograph before they embark on the great adventure. My treasured possessions are a photograph of my mother and sister taken with my nine-month-old brother, and the picture of a girl pal, a school-girl chum, who week by week sends me cheerful letters. A farewell glimpse of these, and I bestow them in a green envelope—one which is not censored by the platoon officer—which I carefully seal and address to my people. There is something extraordinary behind this action, for I cannot possibly conceive myself coming out of the forthcoming engagement unscathed. One would be a fool to hope for so much and the least I expect is a blighty one; hence I have also addressed a Field Post Card, obliterating the formal sentences all but the message, 'I am in hospital, sick. Letter follows.'

At the door of the hostel the sergeant appears, crying, 'Fall in, lads!'

We put on our equipment, take a last look at the room, and file out on to the road. After a brief inspection by the officer, we number, form fours, and march away, knowing that we are going to do a tremendously big thing towards finishing the war. As we march away, our eyes are ablaze with a resolute determination to do our utmost, even if it means giving our lives in the attempt.

Tramp, tramp, tramp.

In the blue-grey light of the September evening we march towards the line, section by section, leaving a gap between each to minimise any damage by an unexpected shelling of the road. My company is leading, and at first the boys are anxious, but spirits begin to soar as they realise they have something big to do.

A voice in front breaks into song, and our platoon officer brightens as he shouts, 'Sing up, lads!' and the song is heartily taken up. After many well-known marching songs we are all feeling more cheerful, and I am happy to be included in this company of youth, for we have been informed that the coming offensive is to be the beginning of the end.

By the side of the road, cages have been erected, and as troops on the roadside cheer as we pass, we call to them that the cages will be full of German prisoners by the time we return.

Although still some distance from the line, there are many large craters blown by enemy shells, some transformed into pools. As we draw near to the line, a conspicuous notice announces, *Road under observation. Drivers make no dust.* Camouflage hides one side of the road. Cigarettes are put out and singing is forbidden.

Further on we halt to receive an additional load. I receive two petrol tins filled with water, and in single file we hurry on, stumbling clumsily because of holes, for the night is now an inky blackness. The extra weight we carry causes many to cry that they can keep the pace no longer. Young Scott is almost doubled up, for he is not much bigger than his pack. I keep murmuring, 'Keep on just as long as you can. Then a little longer,' and then, as far as I am concerned, a miracle happens, for the weight in my hands appears to be lighter, as if the heavy water had run out of the petrol cans.

Keeping touch in the darkness by following the shadow of the man in front, we arrive in the front trench. I still have the tins, and they are full. Back in the trench we know—although it is hardly possible to recognise it, owing to the damage—we take over from the retiring forces, a section at a time, discussing the situation with them in whispers.

'Comfortable apartments, chum. Gas and water laid on.'

I enquire if we have electric light and baths.

'Yes, chum. Turkish,' and as a parting greeting, he whispers, 'You're in for a hot time, Jock—good luck!'

I recognise that I am in the section I occupied last time with the wooden cross over the parapet, but the cross now leans over to one side.

The moon shines through the clouds, machine guns are chattering, and a certain amount of high explosive smoke hangs like a fog, which, together with the Véry lights, are reminders that the war is still on, although we consider this to be 'quiet.' A machine-gunner out on the left is rendering the well-known *Rat-rat-er-rat-rat. Rat-rat!* which provokes some enemy gunner to reply.

There is a gap in the parapet of the next bay which a German gunner is using for target practice, causing us to take a serious interest in this war. We fix the enemy gun from the sparks, and

Preparation

play our Lewis gun, searching for the spot where we judge the aggressive weapon is concealed.

For a time all is quiet and we think we have silenced him, but he opens out again: fire and counter-fire for a time; then all is silent once more.

Such a silence is often sinister, conjuring thoughts of what is going to happen next, but tonight I pick out the constellations. Orion is in the south, and the sparkling brilliance of Sirius causes me wonder. What does God think of this: does He care? The statesmen who hold the destiny of men in their hands never see the wounded out here. When they do visit they see them cheery and happy in a hospital bed, and believe the journalists who write of the glory of war and that the men want to get better quickly and have another pot.

A bombardment starts on our right. Troops are straightening the line, attacking under a smoke screen, beneath a full moon. A little later there is a similar action on our left, then I am relieved from sentry and, squeezing into a tiny shelter under the parados, I go to sleep.

The wall of my shelter is illuminated by the phosphorescent beams of the moon; and waking before dawn I see that I had hung my shrapnel helmet on a leg bone protruding through the side. Other men, and now I, have slept with an unknown soldier.

I am freezingly cold, my limbs are numb, and after an effort to unfasten my belt and slip off my equipment, I free myself from the grave and stand shivering in the trench. MacDonnell is already pacing up and down the duck-boards in an effort to keep warm, so I join him, vigorously flapping my arms across my body, which improves the circulation.

Two men are standing on sentry at each end of the bay, while Scott is resting, too cold to sleep, on the fire step. The other members of the section are in dugouts at the rear of the trench. It is uncomfortably quiet; a cloud passes over the moon, and our small world is plunged into darkness, but the blackout is momentary, as a high wind speedily moves the small cloud onwards, leaving the moon to shed its silver-green light on us. A cock crows in the distance.

'Kick me, Chris,' says MacDonnell, full of surprise. 'Am I standing in a trench or in a country farmyard?'

Another cock answers the call, and one of the sentries, half turning so as to see into the trench, is much perturbed and calls to me, 'Those blasted birds'll give our position away if they keep on screeching like that.'

I do not reply to his remark, as I believe it myself: not that a feathered rooster will inform the enemy of our whereabouts, but it is making a noise, a clarion call, and our tired, frightened and nervy minds hang on to the idea that the cock will arouse the sleeping enemy and cause him to blow us to the moon.

Now a dog barks, the echo ringing across the sleepy and frosty air. The cock crows again, the other bird answers, and another cloud—a much bigger one this time—completely obscures the moon. Silence once again, and MacDonnell and I resume our walking.

A whitish-grey light is gradually appearing in the sky: the moon now is entirely blotted out, heralding the approach of dawn, and once again the call of the cock pierces the air. Suddenly the quietness is broken by a screeching whistle, and a heavy shell lands *Crump! Bang! Wallop!* behind the trench, followed immediately by four more. The sentry turns and stares at me, but says not a word about the cock, although he has his suspicions that the old bird has brought this trouble upon us.

'Stand to! Stand to!' cries the sergeant, and the trench is manned.

Crump! Bang! Crump! Bang!—and the air is filled with high explosives flying along on their journey of hate. The sky changes colour, the diffused greyish-white turning to pale yellow, now a soft pink, and as the clouds roll along, the light becomes a greyish-blue, and the rising sun is shrouded by light clouds. Still the enemy shells fly over and detonate.

'Good morning' having been eloquently observed by the Germans, our artillery, to show no ill feeling, send Fritz a good helping in return.

During the morning we discuss the ethics of 'scrounging' and 'flogging.' Flogging as used in the army vocabulary means thieving and selling for gain. Apparently scrounging is not morally bad. Here we are, living under a perfect socialist regime, the state providing for all, feeding, clothing, housing (if we can call trench life housing), caring for the sick, everything. More or less, we are on equal terms, receiving equal pay and rations. There is no workhouse and we have no paupers. We have no materials with which to build our houses, our dugouts or bivouac,

Preparation

save that lying on the state dumps. In order to provide warmth, we take the fuel that is to hand—the wreckage of broken and ruined buildings, sometimes coal from the dump by the railway when we are travelling behind the line: sometimes we might scrounge a tin of hard biscuits and thus kindle a fire. So if something is required which will provide extra comfort, we do not steal it from another man: we scrounge it—pick it up and use it to good purpose.

Even in such a socialistic state we find some men becoming richer owing to thrift and other causes. The thrifty may not spend so much in drink or tobacco. Other men by their wits are becoming capitalists. They mimic company promoters of the worst kind, and run the Crown and Anchor boards, growing fat on the losses of the weak speculators anxious for quick returns. So it goes on, the individual using his brains—the property which no socialist state can hope to make common—some for the good of the community, others to shift all the hard and tiresome work on the shoulders of the weaker members.

We have this in the army as in civil life. Often we are on short rations, although the full amount has been issued to the supply-source. Go into the village, and you will find army bully beef and other foodstuffs; while on the beds it may be possible to find a blanket not unlike those issued by His Majesty's Government. How did they get there? The answer is, 'A good fairy brought them.'

And so the business goes on, the greedy avaricious few lining their pockets at the expense of others who do not get sufficient nourishment at the best of times.

This afternoon the district is extremely quiet, and I am left with my thoughts. The other men are either reading or writing letters, and the corporal is looking into the wastes of No-man's-land through a periscope. The thoughts of last night recur to me, for like many men in Flanders and elsewhere, I am given to mental arguments in the search for truth.

In my younger days, although for many years in a church choir, I did not trouble much about religion. I was interested in the Old Testament stories, but on the strength of the New Testament and in the light of new experiences I am not able to reconcile the God of the Old Testament to my ideas of a God of Love. All my preconceived ideas are being shattered, and I am steadily and securely rebuilding a greater structure. I looked upon the Old Testament history as literal truth, which now does not fit in with my world. Here it is that Scouting has proved invaluable: it holds something concrete: boyish adventure, and love of God and man and of the whole of God's creation; it has shown me the beauties of the infinite; and those wonderful camps at home are a treasure of memory to fall back upon. They help to erase the scars of the utter desolation surrounding us, and to penetrate the cloud which at present veils the beautiful. Earlier that morning the stretcher-bearer had said that God had revealed Himself through the ages according to man's capacity to understand. Then came the Christian religion when the dual streams of Greek thought and the philosophy of Jewry fused into the new thought of Christianity. He went on to describe the orderly thinking of the Greeks, 'the one and the many', 'unity in diversity', and the religion of the Jews with the belief in a divine plan. Both Plato and Aristotle had enriched the thinking of the early Christian Fathers.

Most fellows out here have no express creed or dogma; but they speak words of cheer when most needed, share comforts, and hasten to help when one is in a tight corner, with no thought of God, yet they have caught a ray from the cross.

The corporal jumps from the fire step, handing the periscope to Blair with orders to look out for prowling Germans. He asks me what I have been thinking about, for he seems to have an uncanny knack of reading faces.

'Nothing much,' is all I can say.

Corporal Edwards smiles and is prepared to wait, adding, 'I know, I've heard that before.'

He is in the humour for a chat, so I continue, saying, 'I've been thinking of the beauty of earth and sky as opposed to all this ugliness. It sort of lifts one up. We're not hopelessly lost yet.'

'It's extraordinary, but I find myself taking interest in the sunrise and sunset, where at home I'd dismiss them with some hackneyed word such as "lovely" or "fine",' answers Corporal Edwards, and adds, 'But I wasn't thinking of beauty just now. I was thinking about this place during the Battle of the Lys last April. At that time I was in the 51st Division. On the 9th April, after a heavy bombardment during which thirty to forty thousand gas shells were fired into Armentieres, eight German divisions attacked on a nine-mile front. We had just come out of the line,

Preparation

but we were quickly drawn into the struggle. Next day the attack spread to the Ypres-Comines canal where the Fourth German Army joined in. Our front was penetrated at Ploegsteert Wood, and the ridge at Messines twice changed hands. Armentieres was surrounded and fell, then Estaires and Merville fell on the eleventh. Neuve Eglise later, and Bailleul on the 15th April, when Hazebrouck was threatened.

'It was hell, I can tell you, and when Kemmel was captured we were compelled to withdraw from the high ground east of Ypres, including Passchendaele Ridge. Many new British and French divisions reinforced the line, mostly boys rushed from the training camps in Blighty.'

'Jerry must have lost heavily too!' I interject.

'Lost! We simply mowed them down, but Kemmel was stormed by German shock troops on the 25th April, with the aid of swarms of low-flying aeroplanes, and that success seriously threatened Ypres. The French defenders of Kemmel had fearful casualties.

'It was touch and go with us, and in less than six weeks from the 21st March the enemy had flung a hundred and forty-one divisions against the combined French and British forces. The fifty-five British Infantry divisions and three Cavalry divisions of Haig's army stayed the attacks of a hundred and nine German divisions, and the third great German campaign in the west had been defeated, but at a terrible cost.'

'The British casualties alone were four hundred thousand killed, wounded and missing, eighty thousand prisoners taken by Fritz, and close on eight hundred guns lost. Fortunately the enemy was also exhausted, and was obliged to stay his hand.'

Now it is our turn to advance against the Germans over the same ground.

During odd intervals, when on duty in the trench, I have been fortunate in getting Blair to talk about himself. He is the eldest of nine children; his brothers and sisters are being cared for by an Institution, owing to bad home influence. His father is living with another woman by whom he has had six children, and his mother is living with another man and has had four more children. Blair has never known a home, and it is not surprising that he has no ideals and no religion. I can only gather that he is a 'determinist', a belief which higher education has almost made extinct.

'If God made me, then He is to blame for everything I do. If this cartridge in the spout of my bondhook,' says Blair, tapping his rifle magazine, 'happens to be a dud, it's not the fault of the bullet but of the maker.'

'That's quite true,' I say, 'but isn't there a difference between you and a cartridge? You have the power, the will, to fire that rifle if you care to. On the other hand, you know that it is orders to fire only in certain circumstances. If you have a desire to fire blindly at anything you see, your actions should be controlled by the knowledge that you must not. The rifle is simply a useless piece of wood without you to cause it to act. God gave you power to create men like yourself, and having this creative power, can you honestly blame God for everything you do wrong? Can you blame Him for your actions which you have the power to control?'

'That's all very well, but I don't believe in a God; and if there is a God, he is responsible for my actions. Goodness is only a myth associated with your God for those who are comfortable. If there is a good God, He will stop all this killing. Your God will do nothing for me. He won't take me away from this and find me a decent home.'

We talk for a considerable time, but Blair remains rigid in his views. What little hope he had has been shattered by the war, and it will be a long process under expert guidance and friendly supervision if he is to find any kind of faith. What he requires is a good home influence. There is a tremendous amount of good in him, and in a very short space of time he has learned to respect the family of the trenches and is less abusive than he was. He is learning the first moral duty of self-mastery and his duty to the family. Perhaps it would prove a blessing if he could get a blighty one when he would come under the care of a good woman nurse who would give him a glimpse of the motherly care that has been denied him.

THE FINAL ADVANCE 1918

In September 1918, the Allies launched a series of offensives along the length of the Western Front:
(1) 26th September: the American First Army and the French Fourth Army attacked on the right between Rheims and the Meuse.
(2) 27th September: the British Third and First Armies attacked between Peronne and Arras.
(3) 28th September (the subject of this narrative): the British Second Army, the Belgian Army and the French Sixth Army—under the command of the King of the Belgians and known as the 'Group Army of Flanders'—attacked on the left between Armentieres and the sea.
(4) 29th September: the French First Army and the British Fourth Army, including two American Divisions, attacked in the right centre between La Fere and Epehy.

The Germans had constructed a series of positions, beginning with the Hindenburg Line in the south, and there were also numerous rivers and canals which the Germans hoped to hold with Super Counter-Attack Divisions; in the event these divisions were not as effective as had been hoped because, instead of concentrating their attack, the Allies threw their punches at a number of different points.

The Group Army of Flanders made a good start on the 28th and recovered the whole of the Ypres Ridge. The Second Army under General Plumer then became right flank guard along the River Lys while the Belgians and French thrust towards Brussels. Owing to heavy rain and mud, the French and Belgian transport system broke down and the advance was held up for a fortnight; for some of this time, my battalion worked on the roads and then went forward again to the Lys in a hurry when the British Second Army became the spearhead with my battalion as reserve. On the Lys, the Flanders Army was again held up until the 28th October when the British Fourth, Third and First Armies successfully dislodged the Germans on the right. The whole Flanders Army Group then went forward to the Scheldt where they came to a halt facing the German Hermann Position—which Hindenburg had ordered to be held for at least eight days.

The advance was resumed on 1st November by the British Fourth, Third and First Armies together with the Americans on the right and was continued until the Armistice.

The enemy offered stiff resistance, chiefly with artillery, machine-gun posts and mortars. Our supplies were hampered by blown up bridges and cratered railway lines; everything had to be rushed forward by General Service wagons and horsedrawn transport—no easy task with our troops thirty miles ahead of the railhead. Rations, ammunition, fodder, medical supplies, pontoons for bridge-building were all a problem; it is a wonder that we managed to advance as quickly as we did. The British Fifth and Second Armies and the other units of the Army Group were held up on the Scheldt until 8th November when they crossed without opposition.

8

The Beginning of the End

It is Friday night, and visitors are arriving, bringing with them machine guns and ammunition. It is not an evening to receive guests, but when a war is on, no account is taken of times, and invitations are seldom given or accepted in this locality. I have heard a rumour that Friday night is bath night. It might have been, but circumstances alter cases, and bath nights are now measured by months. The machine gunners are cheery fellows, and cause a deal of excitement as they talk of the approaching attack. Some are setting the guns, others are sitting on the parapet fixing them in position. The congestion in the trench makes it almost impossible to move, and if a shell detonates here, there will be a big job for the burial party.

The sergeant calls, 'Number Four Platoon to go down for rations.'

We collect ourselves and leave for the road. Our journey is not easy, for we have to climb over lumps of earth where the trench has been blown in. Coming out on to the road, we hurry along to the ration limbers.

'Any *doopang*, Alex?' enquires one of the men carelessly.

'Aye, *beaucoup* bread tonight,' is the cheerful answer.

The limbers are duly unloaded, the contents distributed among the party, and we are ready to return to the trench when—*Whizz-bang, weez-bang* and I hide myself beneath the sack of bread I have on my shoulder, going down on my knees. This is a bit of Jerry's scrap-iron. It comes with a whizz and goes with a bang: time, one-and-a-half seconds, and is the finest thing on earth to sharpen the wits. The mules do not like it and bolt: fortunately their heads have been turned towards home and someone suggests that they have gone to Calais to find a boat. As the shelling ceases, we pick up our loads again and start on the journey to the trench. The enemy searchlights are playing upon the cloudy sky, and as their artillery appears to be more active than usual, I wonder if they anticipate our attack in the morning.

I hear the crack of a gun being fired somewhere in the enemy rear, and now become gradually and painfully aware of an ever-nearing scream through the air, heralding the approach of a 'five-point-nine'—a giant wind-jammer. As it crashes, it makes a hole about a foot-and-a-half deep. Often these shells distribute blighties but this one is harmless.

We resume our journey, and are almost at the corner of the trench when a 'nine-point-two' explodes, and the Hun gives us a fine opportunity for sport as we break the record for the one hundred yards, all because of a nine-point-two, and in the shelter of the trench, we get well down to it, all in a heap, which does not improve the bread I carry.

No blighties are flying about, and we scramble over the broken ground which has once been a trench and deliver the groceries.

'Thank God that job's done,' murmurs Blair with a sigh of relief.

After a time the corporal brings the rations for our section, which we prematurely consume, as the corporal suggests we will have enough to carry without taking rations over the top; in any case it is a wise precaution, for we might not have the opportunity later.

It is close upon midnight and a new day—Saturday 28th September—will shortly begin. Lieutenant Jacques appears and reminds us of our orders, and informs us the Queen of the Belgians will open the attack by firing the first gun, the signal for the barrage to commence from northern Belgium, working south on a four-and-a-half mile front.

'It'll be easy at first,' says the officer. 'We will walk behind the barrage and, as we advance, the barrage will lift. Keep just behind the "lifting barrage" and all will be well. The machine gunners will also cover us with a barrage from this trench. We are now going over the top to take up our position in No-man's-land. Come on, boys!'

The officer leads our silent advance to the jumping-off place. Here we lie down, cramped on the shell-torn ground, and the cold is intense. If we move, the pick or shovel will ring against the shrapnel helmet. After a time, the fellow next to me snores, and I pinch him to keep him awake. I am falling asleep and the corporal rouses me. The fight against sleep in such a dangerous position is terribly difficult.

Something hard is projecting from the ground and sticking into my thigh, and I carefully manoeuvre to remove the object: I am not able to displace it for I discover it is the skeleton bone of a man long since buried under the clay. Shells have burst near the grave and disturbed the remains.

After a wait of five hours, the officer is seen approaching, and stopping in front of us, for he has come from the direction of the enemy line. 'I'm darned sorry, boys, but I couldn't get the rum up, and in a quarter of an hour we go.'

I tremble upon thinking what I can do when I eventually rise, for I am almost frozen, my teeth are chattering, and my limbs are stiff with cramp and the icy coldness of the ground. I do not feel at all capable of launching an attack upon the enemy two hundred yards away.

I watch and wait for the offensive to begin, my heart beats wildly and I have a sense of suffocation in my throat; my brain becomes excited, and I ask myself what is in store. What a futile question: for how can I possibly know? One minute we are thinking and talking or jesting; the next we might be in eternity. But the prospect of death does not trouble or alarm me, although to come out without a scratch seems most unlikely.

Is it the cold or the excitement which makes me shiver?

A fearful quietness overwhelms us, causing anxious suspense. Daylight is beginning to peep, but the sky is overcast and cloudy—a portent of rain. How slowly the minutes tick, especially the last, as I wait holding my breath.

At last! *Crack! Bang!*

Thunder and lightning! Up we jump, and walk behind the bursting shells. It is devastating, but to me it is also interesting. I look back. 'Hell!' I exclaim, as I see a pillar of fire behind me, whilst I am confronted with fire and the explosion of shells rending the earth, throwing up fragments of clay as a fountain sends up spray. The noise is bewildering: the rumble of the guns, the chatter of the machine guns, and the hissing of the bullets as they speed over and around, the shouting of men, and the cries as a man falls down wounded by shrapnel or machine gun bullets.

Despite this inferno and the fact that I possess all my faculties,

An observation balloon on Pilckem Ridge

Digging wounded out of a collapsed regimental aid post

Artillery observation post near Ypres, August 1918

not having been doped with alcohol, I am not now afraid, and the whirl of the machine gun bullets around me concerns me less than rain might. In my mind's eye I see the image of my family as they appear in the photograph I carry; and before me also flashes the face of the girl whose photograph I have. And the memory of these loved ones spurs me onwards, for they are my England: it is for them that I am fighting this battle. My one thought is to help in winning through, as this battle will be a deciding factor in bringing the war to a speedy conclusion.

Corporal Edwards is some yards ahead, and as I quicken my steps, a yawning cavity, fully twenty feet deep and not less than ten yards in circumference, appears before me. I attempt to surmount this chasm by making a circular movement, and simultaneously feel a twinge of pain in one of my fingers of the right hand, caused by a piece of shrapnel, the blast causing me to slip down into the crater. In a fever of anxiety I hastily scramble to the top, and hearing the shouts of the corporal who is waving his rifle frantically, he being nearest to the enemy, I run towards him.

'Look out! Machine gun nest!' he cries, but his warning is a second too late, for I run headlong into the defenders of the stronghold, and my kilt is caught on the wire entanglements. Here I am held like a fly in the web of a spider, held so close to the gunner that if I stretch forward my hand I could touch him. The bullets from the machine gun are speeding away before my eyes but fortunately the gunner either does not notice me in the confusion, or he is unable to traverse his gun beyond an angle of forty-five degrees.

'Get down, you damned fool!' roars the corporal, who thinks I am attacking the gunner.

'How can I? I'm trying to get unstuck!' I angrily retort. I tug desperately at my kilt while beads of perspiration flow down my face. With death staring at me, I feel as if my end has come, when with a final tug, my kilt parts company, and I am free but with only half a kilt. With a sigh of relief I duck beneath the breastworks in order to recover and to take stock. The guns continue furiously to spit forth their deadly pieces of lead, and on looking up, I see over a hundred Germans holding up their hands and screaming '*Kamerade!*'

Crouching beneath the protective earthworks, my section bomb and snipe, but without any apparent effect upon the enemy gunners holding the mine crater. I hear someone shout, 'We'll have to retire!'

Immediately the voice of the corporal is heard above the uproar and tumult of bursting shells, trench mortars and machine gun fire, 'Who the hell says retire? You don't know anything about bloody warfare!' After which outburst his voice is lost to me in the confused noises. The lance-corporal is next to me, and having thrown over his hand-grenades, suddenly yells above the deafening roar, 'Hell! I've forgotten to pull the pins out!'

The corporal hears him, and shouts in answer,

'You barmy devil! What the 'ell d'you think you're doing? Jerry'll throw them back at us. Call yourself a soldier! You ought to be . . .'

I hand two Mills bombs to the corporal, thus calming the stormy tempest of abuse, saying, 'Don't forget to take the pins out.'

Events have moved rapidly, and all these strange things have occurred in the space of a few seconds. After what appears an interminable time we find that only one enemy gun is in action. A fair young fellow is standing and firing into our troops, intent upon holding on to the end despite the fact that the terrified wretches behind him are waiting to be captured.

'He's a brave fellow!' cries the corporal. 'I was hoping we could capture him. A man like that doesn't deserve to die.'

I share the corporal's admiration for the German, who is one of the bravest men I have encountered. If we could only force a way through to his flank and get behind him we might be able to save him, but that is impossible as his gun is the key to the situation. We shall be held up until that gun is put out of action.

Our second wave now reinforces us, and I am attracted by a man caught in the impenetrable tangle of wire. I put down my rifle and, with a pair of wire cutters, work frantically to cut him free. Having got him free, I turn to recover my rifle, and find it has been shattered beyond further use. Seizing another left by an incapacitated man, I join the corporal. The Germans behind are still crying '*Kamerade*'—having discarded their steel helmets and gas respirators together with their arms and equipment, but the gun on the brink of the crater rattles away, the hatless fair-haired German standing in an inferno of bursting shells and hand grenades.

'Where's the Lewis gun?' shouts the corporal; but our Lewis

gunner has been killed and the gun lies somewhere on the ground. I hastily look round for a Lewis gun, but before I can grasp one, I am arrested by a runner who has joined us, enquiring if I am 'Four Platoon?'

'Yes,' I reply.

The runner hands a sandbag to me and vanishes as mysteriously as he appeared; the corporal, perceiving the action, calls out to me that the bag contains a jar of rum. 'You stick to that bag, and never mind the war. Keep close to me,' he orders.

Suddenly the German gun ceases and away our platoon go, passing the enemy who have surrendered, as prisoners do not concern us: we have to get to our objective and get dug in. On my way I decide to take no risks and pick up a Lewis gun I find beside a dead man; hanging tenaciously to the rum jar, I collect some pans of ammunition. We advance too far and an officer orders us to withdraw to the line of our objective.

This is a welcome order, for Corporal Edwards was certain we had advanced far enough, and pointed to a ruined Piccadilly Farm on the right. He was so certain, that he argued with a sergeant from another platoon with such vehemence that it became a slanging match. This sergeant was pressing us to advance further, and I was amused when our excited but competent corporal shouted, 'We stay put. You're only a bloody cook-house sergeant.'

Further abuse from the sergeant, who bellowed, 'You're scared. There's no Germans for miles. We can take the ridge.'

The corporal retorted angrily, 'No Germans for miles!—that's why you want to go. Advance on your own if you like, and you'll find yourself in front of our protective barrage.'

It was then that the officer approached and informed us we had over-run our objective by approximately twenty yards. What a leader we have in Corporal Edwards!

The rain is pouring down, and the ground already a quagmire, making it impossible to consolidate by digging a trench: the only alternative for the platoon is to take cover in two shell holes half-filled with water.

Airmen fly over, looking for the line, and we signal with the metal discs supplied for that purpose. The protective barrage then commences, the shells detonating in a line in front of our position, and almost simultaneously the enemy rain a barrage of shells a few yards behind us.

We clean the Lewis gun as best we can and prepare for a counter-attack. I remove the cork from the rum jar and each man takes a canteen lid full of the burning liquid, which we sorely need, as our feet are now well under the water and we are numbed with cold. Here we are with only a few francs between us—about two hundred—and the irony is that the money is worthless, as the food and cigarettes we require are not to be obtained at any price. I share this shell hole with Corporal Edwards, Robert Scott and another new fellow, Dennis Craig. In the other shell hole are the lance-corporal and three others, making eight men belonging to our platoon who are at present accounted for.

It continues to rain, and the water in the shell hole is steadily rising, which so concerns us that we are having a heated argument over the vexed question of whether shell fire bursts rain clouds. The tension is relieved as the enemy put up three observation balloons, causing Craig to exclaim, 'Look yonder: old Fritz is going to counter-attack.'

We prepare for the counter-attack by taking the cork out of the rum jar, as we are getting wetter and colder, and the rum counter-attacks the chill; now we are ready to hold on to the end, even if a hundred German divisions charge down upon us.

The humming of a British plane is heard, flying low, and passing above us it soars forward towards the German observation balloons, making a sudden dart and charging into the balloons one by one, setting them on fire; then the airman soars heavenward to escape the enemy anti-aircraft shells and, turning his nose in the direction of our lines, escapes through the small black puffs of smoke which encircle him. We enjoy this action, for we have no desire to remain under the observation of the enemy. After a time, however, the Germans put up another balloon, and the airman returns and sends it blazing to the ground, the observers descending safely on parachutes. Still another balloon is ascending, and the plane describes a circle and returns to the attack, but the balloon is hauled down before the plane reaches it.

This interesting contest has caused us to forget for a time our discomforts, and we laugh and applaud.

'Hastie Mac', who is in the other shell hole, crawls over to us for a mess tin portion of rum, and on returning becomes so brave that he is a nuisance and a danger to us all; Corporal Edwards is compelled to raise his rifle and threaten Hastie with

The Beginning of the End

sudden death if he persists in standing up and waving his arms in a boastful attempt to attract the enemy.

The Germans hoist up another observation balloon, and in a few minutes the British airman returns, hovers for a second or two, then darts for the balloon. But alas, the plane is caught in the fire of the enemy anti-aircraft guns and comes down in flames.

This episode lowers our spirits, and we discover that there is still water in the shell hole, that we are hungry, with no prospect of obtaining food until nightfall at the earliest, that we could enjoy a smoke, but the cigarettes in our pockets are saturated with the rain, and, further, that our bodies are blue with cold.

We gaze languidly at each other and force a smile as Scott forlornly exclaims, 'This is the wreck of the Hesperus, and I'm the blooming wreck.'

What a frightful collection of wretches we are! Hose tops are resting on the tops of our boots and are caked with mud; kilts are hanging at all angles; legs are plastered with mud, and here and there a tiny tint of red showing through the dirt tells the tale of the wire-infested area we have recently fought through.

'A perfect picture of a soldier,' remarks Scott in derision.

As the day wears on, it becomes certain that the enemy will not attempt a counter-attack, for fresh British divisions are already storming his lines.

I miss MacDonnell, but he may have got lost, and will perhaps appear later in the day, so I am not inclined to worry at present. We talk of various episodes of army life, and make comparison with our present position and other places, some worse, some better. The corporal has been out here for a long time, and has gone through the real hell of Flanders, and his reminiscences help to pass away the time and keep our thoughts from dwelling upon our discomforts.

'I often think of the thousands of bodies,' says the corporal, 'broken and battered, lying beneath the ground. Some have wooden crosses, others rest in unknown graves, yet each has carried a cross whether he knew it or not. Somehow their spirits seem near to me.'

'Death appears different to what I once thought it was.' says Craig. 'Now, I think of death as the quitting of one experience into a new life. It's incomprehensible, but I feel it all the same.'

'We owe a tremendous debt to those men who came out here

in the beginning,' says the corporal. 'They struggled against fearful odds—both the weather and the enemy. I can only go as far back as '17, and that was bad enough. That is Passchendaele over there on our left, a village in peace-time; it was lost in the First Battle of Ypres. In '17 it was stormed by the Canadians under dreadful weather conditions. From the ridge there is an extensive view of the Belgian plain—ranging as far as Ostend on the coast on a clear day—so it was quite a strategic position. But during that battle the weather was against us and Passchendaele stands out in my mind as a symbol of heroic, almost superhuman effort; of strategic failure but of splendid endurance under the most wretched conditions known in war.

'I remember at Messines,' continues Corporal Edwards, his mind wandering from one sector to another, 'the ridge is now strewn with fragments of pill-boxes. On 7th June, 1917, after the heaviest bombardment ever and the explosion of nineteen enormous mines, the reverberations of which were heard in England, the ridge was attacked by General Plumer's Second Army and captured with over seven thousand prisoners and sixty-seven guns. The largest mine crater is at Sparbroekmolen, about one mile south-west of Wytschaete, and it has a diameter of a hundred and forty yards.'

'It must have been a colossal task,' interrupts Craig.

'Indeed it was. The mines took eighteen months to construct, thousands of galleries were driven, and a million pounds of explosives were used.'

'This might have been our lot at home,' says Scott. 'And we must thank those who have gone before. It's a debt which none of us can ever forget.'

'And yet, such debts have been forgotten,' the corporal reminds us.

Darkness is creeping upon us, drawing to a close this wretched day, but we are faced with an even more uncomfortable night, for it is utterly dark, and the rain continues unceasingly. Several enemy machine guns are active, and Scott braves the bullets in order to have a little sleep: getting up out of the water hole, he lies down on his stomach on the slimy ground, and is soon asleep.

It is a long weary night, and several men have been taken from the other shell holes suffering from trench feet. It cannot be

The Beginning of the End

long before the dawn, now, when rations are brought to us. Rations do arrive, and we have bread in abundance, cheese and jam and cigarettes, but we must wait for a smoke until the day breaks.

We have the rations for the full platoon, but only eight of us are so far accounted for. Our sergeant has been killed at the crater—and others, we know—but for the remainder it is not certain whether they are killed or wounded.

The stretcher-bearer joins us in the feast, relating how many bearers have been tending the wounded and dying left on the battlefield. All day long and through the night he has been ministering to the helpless while we have been stuck in this shell hole, and he is drunk with tiredness. He tells us how he picked up one of our lance-corporals still living with thirty-six machine gun bullets in his body, but he is dead probably now, although the hospital staffs have performed some miracles of healing and it might just be possible to save him.

Having eaten with us, the stretcher-bearer continues on his way, for he only dropped in on us to enquire if all were safe, and we have heard a cry in another shell hole, at which he hastens for a fellow needs him.

Before sunrise another attack is made by our troops who are fresh, we remaining in our position. They storm the enemy positions, advancing from both ends of our line and then closing in, thus covering our front and leaving us reserve troops. This attack is successful, and as the morning sun glitters through the clouds, our General appears, with Brigade Major Bonham Carter, and shouts that he is proud of our achievement and that we will soon be relieved.

9

Loving Your Enemy

War is a mixture of love and hate. The individual German seems different to the ruthless Huns at the rear who wage war in safety and look upon the men as cannon fodder.

'We can help a German when he's down and out,' says Scott, as we stand in a quagmire, smoking. 'But can we think well of these warlords who sank the *Lusitania*, executed Nurse Cavell and destroyed towns which need not have been destroyed? What about Bapaume? That town had to be evacuated by the Germans, and not a shell ever hit the town, but the Hun ruthlessly bombed and mined every house and building in the place. The Town Hall was mined, and blew up as our troops entered. That was wanton destruction. There was no necessity for it. Why did he do it? Why did he send gas over?'

'And the *Lusitania*, with all those innocent people on board,' adds Craig.

'Quite true,' replies the corporal. 'But that submarine officer blundered—for blunder it was: it brought America into the war, and their fresh troops are now pouring into France to our aid.'

'What about the murder of Nurse Cavell?' enquires Scott, and the corporal replies, 'The guilt of that crime rests upon some commander. The German higher command ought never to have allowed such a thing to happen.'

'What do you think of the destruction of towns?' asks another.

The corporal pauses to light a cigarette, then: 'The enemy aims at the British troops at their heels rather than at the buildings. If a beautiful church or other edifice is destroyed, it might be that an enemy suspects the building is being used for observation purposes, or gun emplacements. No doubt it sometimes happens that towns and villages are wantonly shelled, in which case it is devilish. I agree that in many ways the Huns have not played the game as we see it, and in war the only effective way is to retaliate. Gas we cannot suffer in silence, and it is necessary to use the same weapon in order to teach the enemy that gas is not a healthy thing to have floating about the atmosphere.'

'Hear, hear!' exclaims Craig.

Our discourse ends as the stretcher-bearer approaches with his colleague bearing a young German. The bearers, after constant trudging through the mud during the past twenty-four hours, are feeling the effects of their laborious task, and they place their charge gently on the ground in front of us and breathe a sigh of exhaustion.

The German is wounded in the stomach and is in great pain, which he bears patiently. He cries, shivers and calls for 'wazzer.' We moisten his lips, and gently pour a few drops of water into his mouth, and he smiles. We ask if he can stand a smoke, at the same time showing him a cigarette. He makes no sound, and a cigarette is lit for him and placed between his lips. The lonely, wretched man is not able to smoke, and the cigarette falls on to his tunic. We ask his age. Eighteen. And Scott curses war, that chaps of his age should be fighting and dying; and Scott is not quite nineteen himself.

It is good that we can sympathise with this German boy, with no thought of ourselves. Love is strong, and we cannot help but love the wretched, lonely boy.

To give the bearers a brief rest, Scott and I help to carry the wounded fellow. The long journey over the quagmire, round shell craters and over tangles of barbed wire, is proving a burden to us in spite of the fact that four of us carry. Each time we slip, our hearts beat wildly, and we feel anguished at causing our wounded prisoner additional pain. After a painful and hazardous trudge, we leave our charge with the RAMC unit who render further aid before sending him down to hospital.

On our return we pass the crater, and find the body of the German gunner who fought so gallantly. His fair hair is parted down the centre, and the only mark on him is a bullet hole through the temple. I offer a prayer over the body and feel certain the others have joined in this silent tribute. It is a sin that good men like him should be slaughtered because a world has not found Christ. His gun has probably killed our beloved sergeant and other friends, but we do not think of this: we only know the gunner has tried to do his duty, as we are attempting to do, and no doubt has said prayers to the same God we call Father; and it is certain that he has left some heartbroken soul in Germany to mourn for him.

There will be many brave hearts at home enduring terrible anxiety, sorrow and torture of mind because of today. We are not the only bodies to feel the hardships of war. It is Sunday, and folk all over Europe will be attending divine service and praying for peace. Sunday is all the same out here; but still at times our confused minds will dwell for a second or two upon another picture, far remote from the war, but nevertheless intermingled with this dreadful reality, through the power of the spirit which knows no bounds. It is refreshing to hear the glad sound of the church bells once again, and to visualise the people going to service, and to listen to the music of the organ, and feel the prayers of loved ones coming by wireless into our hearts. Had we not experienced an English Sunday, nor learned a little about Christ, this desolation and awful hideousness would drive us mad. The churches may have failed in some things, but at least they have handed down the gospel of Christ.

A party of engineers engaged on searching for mines and rendering the explosive monsters ineffective, pause in their dangerous duty to hold cheerful converse with us. They have found and extracted over a hundred and fifty mines in this area. All the German dugouts have been thoroughly explored and made safe, and in cases where German wounded have been found, these engineers have carried them out to await the stretcher-bearers.

This place is alive with stretcher-bearers, and many of the parties are composed entirely of Germans who have taken part in the action of yesterday and this morning. They are patrolling the recent battlefield, picking up both British and German wounded and taking them down to the aid posts. Thus under the ensign of the Red Cross, friend and foe alike are working together to succour the wounded.

It is now about midday and one of our officers blows his whistle. Eight of our platoon fall in for the company roll call. MacDonnell is among the missing.

We leave the Lewis guns and ammunition on the roadside to be picked up by the transport, for it is as much as we can do to carry ourselves and rifles. Footsore, we lounge along, and I am not yet certain that I will not suffer from trench feet, for I can scarcely put my feet to the ground.

It is a sad tramp back to billets, devoid of glory: just a handful of tired men slowly dragging themselves along the muddy road: but the hearts of those men are unconquerable.

The 'cages' erected on the side of the road are filled with a tragic crowd of German prisoners, and I believe they pity us as we go by.

There is no singing as we march down to the rest billets, for we are tired, and caked in mud. We slouch along in it, and it seems impossible to get away from it: mud, mud, everything is mud. We eat it in our food, and it is there in our drinks. We sleep in it, dream of it, and thousands of men have been drowned in the sea of mud which surrounds the Salient.

No singing—although a victory has been won. We trudge on, led by Lieutenant Jacques, thoughts twirling round like a dream not of this world. Majestic minds have departed as payment to rid a world of hostility: a great victory—thousands of prisoners captured. Yet we cannot sing.

Passing a ruined house demolished by incessant shell fire, we see a tiny thing of beauty flourishing amidst this desolation. In the shell-torn garden the grasses have formed a shroud, nature has triumphed over man's vindictiveness, and standing valiantly like sentinels are several magnificent bright red poppies, graceful in their simplicity.

Arriving at Ouderdom, we enter our old billet. A large mail is waiting, but many of the parcels and letters have arrived too late: the letters are returned; but parcels are opened and the contents shared.

It is quiet tonight in the billet, for part of the family is missing, and our platoon singer is not with us. I saw him during the advance, on his knees, and did not realise he was dead until I placed my hand upon his shoulder.

The stretcher-bearer comes in and enquires if he can do anything for us. I show him my finger which has been hit by a piece of shrapnel. The tip was almost hanging off when the accident happened, but the mud formed a cast and hardened. Nothing can be done now and I am kindly assured that in a short time I will have a poisoned finger; so I retire for the night.

In the morning I wake feeling stiff in all my joints, but with a cold sponge followed by gentle massage, I am beginning to feel fit again. The cleaning of our muddy clothing and equipment

March to Armistice

keeps us engaged during the greater part of the morning. News is brought that the Belgians have captured Passchendaele, and on all fronts the Germans are retreating. Reinforcements now come up and our platoon is made up to part strength. Some of the men are new, but others have come from the hospitals, having been wounded in previous actions.

After lunch we parade for a bath and receive a clean change of underclothing. Now, a visit to the quartermaster and we are finally re-equipped, which produces a pleasant effect, and we feel fresh and look like proper soldiers.

Having spent a restful night in billets, we prepare to march after the retreating enemy. We are fresh: it is surprising what a change a day's rest and a bath and new clothing have made. The discomforts and hardships of two days ago are almost entirely obliterated from our memories, in the new venture before us. It is a fine crisp morning, and we march across the shell-torn ground which has recently been in German occupation. Such a dump! Shells, mines, rifles, all kinds of guns from machine guns to heavy howitzers; boxes of bombs, Véry lights, smashed-up limbers, wire, and numerous pill-boxes. Pausing for a rest on one of the ridges, we look down upon the desolate town of Ypres dominating the Salient. The flame from the discharge of one of our guns is seen somewhere near the town, and we realise the advantage the Germans had in holding this position. Little wonder that the total of British casualties in the Ypres Salient exceed those on any other front. But for the courage and determination and sacrifice of our countrymen, Ypres would have fallen long ago; and what then of England?

At Messines we are ravenous, but with no food, and the company cookers reported to be stuck in the mud somewhere. We are stranded.

I go forward to a pill-box, intent on exploring the gloomy portals of the underground cavern, but the stench is insufferable, and I leave whatever spoils there may be to some other individual with an impaired sense of smell.

A few shells are bursting on the road, and creeping nearer to us. They are heavy shells, and the splinters of iron expand outwards for a considerable distance: one detonates fifty yards away, causing me to fall to the ground, not without alarm. I have my rifle slung on my shoulder, and feel a push, but take no further notice. As the commotion subsides, I discover the wooden part round the top has been blown away, and the barrel dented. The officer says I am a 'lucky devil.' This calls for a new rifle.

After a meal consisting of three hard biscuits and a little bully beef, but with no hot drink, as the cooker is still sunk in the mud, we move forward and take up a position in reserve.

A night and part of today has been spent in this position in reserve, and as dusk is approaching, we march downwards in the direction of Wulverghem. We are tired, hungry and dirty, with no prospects of food, when we halt and in the darkness enter the roomy cattle trucks attached to an engine with steam up. The train rumbles along in the darkness for hours and we have no idea where we are being taken to, or what. Suddenly we are aroused as the trucks jolt against each other and the train pulls up. Ordered to disentrain, we have the shock of our lives to find that we are only at Hell Fire Corner.

We later discover the reason for these haphazard moves: the torrential rain had bogged down transports; roads were impassable. The French and Belgian transport system broke down completely, holding up any further advance for the time being. This also gave the Germans a breather. Near Hell Fire Corner we try to sleep on large tarpaulin sheets spread across the road.

Time soon passes, then we hurriedly make our exit from the road to allow the transport wagons to creep on their journey linewards.

On the plain between the road and the ridge is a battery of field guns, and these have been active all the time we have been endeavouring to obtain sleep.

Breakfast over—such as it is—we are detailed for working on the roads, our services in the line not being required. It is freezingly cold, and as fast as we shovel the liquid earth off the road, it pours back again. Shells continually explode in this district, which calls for the painful exercise of constant ducking, and our knees are caked with mud.

Before dusk we leave work, and build a bivouac for the night. Scott and I scrounge corrugated iron and old duckboards, and erect a comfortable weather-proof shelter, but totally inadequate to withstand shelling, and before turning in I watch with interest the flashes from the signal lamps on the ridge.

In the morning Scott informs me there has been a raid by enemy bombing planes during the night, resulting in several casualties to our men. I am unable to convince Scott that I have slept undisturbed by the raid; but I am thankful that I have, for there is nothing more nerve-destroying to me than to sit through a bombing attack listening to the whirling scream of the bombs as they ride through the air. I would submit to any amount of shelling rather than find myself in the midst of an air raid.

'I know the major's brother,' says Scott, confiding in me. 'He lives near to my place at home—a good-natured happy-go-lucky fellow, not caring two pins for anyone. He's a great friend of my family. I've told Mother that his brother is our Second-in-Command.'

Scott is shivering in the cold, in the process of exterminating lice on his shirt. His little body is covered with blood, a ghastly sight.

'What a mess you're in!' I exclaim. 'You ought to report sick. If you're not careful you'll be having blood-poisoning.'

'I can't help it. The little devils eat me to death, and irritate so much that I scratch and scratch. What else can a fellow do?'

'Get attention, and the sooner the better,' I add.

'Look!' exclaims Scott. 'The major—and he's coming this way. Here goes!'

Scott dives into the dugout to make himself respectable. The major comes towards me and, after acknowledging my salute, asks 'Is Scott in your platoon?'

'Yes, sir, he's in the bivouac.'

'Scott!' commands the major, and a head peeps out of the shelter. 'I want you for a minute, Scott.'

Putting on his tunic, Scott walks away with Major Kedie. In a short time he returns all smiles: he has been offered a job in the Quartermaster's Stores: he will sleep beneath blankets at night, have a sufficiency of food and be excused going into action.

'Good luck, Scottie!' I say. 'And don't forget your old pal. When do you leave?'

'In about two days,' he answers.

We fall in and march away to spend another dreary day working on the roads, and somehow I would prefer the front line. Rations are scarce, and I am inordinately hungry. The battalion canteen is empty save for a few tins of boot polish. What irony! Useless boot polish, and not a crumb of a biscuit for almost empty stomachs.

We finish work in the afternoon, and Scott and I amble forth on a foraging expedition. After a tedious journey through the mud we sight a Canadian canteen, the object of our search. Outside is a crowd of soldiers, and as we push forward, a voice is heard crying:

'What about the old hook—the lucky old sergeant-major.'

This is the Crown and Anchor board, well known to the gambling fraternity, but unknown to me before I arrived in France. The 'banker' shuffles the dice, and afterwards rakes in the money. It is a fascinating game and we decide to risk our five francs on a flutter, for we have visions of taking back more biscuits and cigarettes than five francs will purchase. Down goes our money on the Heart, and in a fever we await the result of the dice. We lose.

Why didn't we visit the canteen first and make certain of something to eat and smoke?

Wet, sticky and muddy, we tumble our hungry, tired and miserable bodies into the shelter to rest or think or sleep until the next day.

It is raining this morning, and the pangs of hunger still gnaw beneath the centre button of my tunic, but it is useless reflecting upon the folly of last night. Things are bad enough as they are.

We pack up, and prepare to remove to an unknown destination. The rain continues and the drops of water, much bigger than English rain drops, beat a tattoo on our helmets, then run down our waterproof capes on to our bare legs.

The mud on the road is deep enough to hide our boots, which is not really as bad as it might, but in parts it gets deeper and stickier. We splash through this café-au-lait substance, and with each step a fresh supply of the treacle-like liquid settles upon our legs and clothing, making us miserably uncomfortable.

Rambling over the hills at home I would not have troubled about the rain and mud would not have concerned me, for I would be heading for some particular rendezvous, there to rest by the fireside of a country cottage, consuming ham and eggs and large quantities of tea, and pleasantly chatting while clothing dried out before the roaring homely fire; then a peaceful smoke and a wash, afterwards continuing the walk with ease and comfort. I would be mentally refreshed by the beauty of the countryside and the invigorating walk. Here, beauty has been disfigured by the hand of man, and thousands of khaki-clad humans are going forward in the same coloured mud.

One of the men yells the phrase of a well-known war poster, 'Remember Belgium.'

'We'll never forget it,' another dolefully answers.

Passing a despatch rider struggling with his motor cycle which refuses to move through the thick mud, our fellows shout to him, 'Why don't you get a blooming horse?' and the harassed DR looks anything but comfortable.

Having crawled along for an hour we halt on the side of the road for a rest, which is not very satisfying, as we have to stand. On the side of the road are scores of carcases of mutilated horses and mules. What a pitiable sight they make. I have always looked upon a horse as a noble animal, and to see them battered and mangled by shell-fire sickens me.

'I don't think there's a living creature under the sun which isn't brought into the war,' says one man.

'It certainly looks like it,' I reply.

We resume our march and as motor transport wagons pass a fountain of mud is showered upon us; each time this happens, our souls are sent to perdition on account of the oaths we utter. A familiar sight on this road is a wagon stuck in the mud, immovable, surrounded by gangs of men with jacks helping to raise it.

The rain is still pouring unceasingly, and we feel too miserable to sing. It is not comforting if we do, for any minute we are in danger of receiving a large splash of the coffee-coloured fluid, completely discolouring our faces, and the only amusement we can indulge in are humorous utterances.

'Your King and Country need you,' bawls one of the men, referring to a war recruiting poster.

'Why the 'ell then doesn't our country keep us if we're so much needed, instead of putting us on foreign service?' exclaims another man.

The banter brings us to a reasonable state of cheerfulness despite the rain and mud.

'Join the Army and see the world' is the chorus of another fellow, which brings the rapid answer, 'Join the Army and see the next world.'

We observe a board bearing the words, *This is Wytschaete.*

'So this is White Sheet?'

'Where?' comes the chorus from the weary marchers, for the village has entirely disappeared into the mud.

'What is Wytschaete?' a chap in front of me enquires.

Limbers held up by mud on the Menin Road and supplies transferred to pack-mules, 29th September 1918

RAMC and German prisoners attending to the wounded

French cavalry resting in 29th Division lines, unable to advance further

'The name of our cat,' is the ready answer.

The extraordinary feature about the character of a British soldier is that he is never so humorous as when 'up against it' and absolutely fed up. It is the humour which helps us to stick it out here, and the best jokes resulting in side-splitting laughter are created when men are well on the borders of pessimism. I have heard the story of one man who had the misfortune to fall into a shell hole up to the neck in icy cold water, and the only word he uttered was 'Blow!' That is only a story.

The rain is ceasing a little, and we take the road to Kemmel, where we build a shelter on the side of the famous hill to house us for the night, for we are now reserve troops.

After a fairly decent sleep we awake this morning as Jerry commences to pound the hill with scrap iron and a huge 'Johnson' lands with a deafening roar and thundering concussion by the side of me. Our new sergeant, two others and myself are flung half way down the hill, and I see all the angels waiting for me at the gates of heaven. I have almost reached the apogee of human life when the cataclysm of earth and iron ceases to whirl. The trembling ground quietens, and slowly and painfully I pick myself up and find my anatomy intact. Dennis Craig is nursing a bleeding knee, and laughingly exclaims, 'That shell was made of bricks!'

Sure enough, tiny fragments of red brick surrounds the wound.

The mules are harnessed to the cooker on the road below, bringing the breakfast. They speedily bolt for a safe spot, taking our bacon and tea with them. A mule may be stupid but he knows how to evacuate the danger zone.

After painting Craig's knee with iodine and tying on a dressing, we slowly mount the hill, there to discover that my bivouac has disappeared, and my new rifle and Lewis gun ammunition have been blown to blazes. There is a gaping crater not three yards from where I had been standing, and the pieces of earth which had been blown out must weigh over two hundredweight. More than three hundred yards away, many of our men have been wounded by the same shell.

Five of these thunderbolts have now dropped and detonated among us, which is about the full ration for one gun, and the enemy gunners must give it a rest.

Peace once more, but only bread and shock for breakfast; I am thirsting for a drink of hot tea, but the cooker has not yet been captured—the object had a flying start, for its attendants were struck motionless by the explosion of the shells.

The corporal receives orders to leave us in order to take a 'Special Course' behind the line, lucky fellow. He takes the high road, and we the low road.

The sun is shining, which puts us in a cheerful frame of mind. Around Mount Kemmel the roads are strewn with German dead, and many British bodies are scattered about the muddy earth with only the clothing holding the decomposed bodies together. Taking the road through Lindenhook we fall out for a rest near Spy Farm. Finding a dry mound of earth, I squat, light a cigarette, and after two or three puffs, look around and discover scores of khaki-clad bodies almost undiscernible, spread over the muddy ground. Going through the pockets of a corpse, I find a letter almost fallen into dust of decay, but with part of an address in Somerset faintly decipherable. With infinite care I hand the pieces of crumbling paper to my officer who places them in his wallet, and will later dispatch the remnants of a love letter—the only means of identification—to records. Thus some long-suffering people at home will be acquainted with the news that their dearly loved boy, reported as missing, is indeed dead, and their tortured minds will perhaps be comforted. The worst news a soul can receive is that their boy is missing: it might mean anything, and the human mind in times of anguish is sometimes unkind and prone to weave pictures of the lost one wandering in some obscure prison, or, what is worse, confined to a life of slavery, brutally illtreated, living, yet unknown to anyone. This boy will rest in an unknown soldier's grave, for the envelope addressed to him has long since faded into dust. He will be buried with an inscription upon his cross, 'Known only unto God.'

Near Hollebeke we prepare to spend the night in some old trenches before moving on to Passchendaele tomorrow.

We meet the Royal Irish who are going up the line. The two Irish divisions, 16th and 36th, were kept as far as possible apart until after the Somme, when both were sent to a quiet part of the line from Kemmel to opposite Messines where they came for the first time into contact and there made friends. Captain Willie Redman of the 18th Royal Irish, who was killed on the ridge between Wytschaete and Messines in July 1917, was entertained at the Ulster Headquarters, and the Ulster Headquarters were entertained by him. In the winter of '16 Redman was taken out of the line and attached to brigade headquarters, but when the offensive on the Messines ridge came in sight, he insisted that he must be allowed to go over with his regiment, and obtained leave to join the third wave of the attack. He pushed on into the front line before the mines went up that July morning and, going over, a bullet struck him. His regiment was shoulder to shoulder with the Ulstermen; the stretcher-bearers who picked him up were Ulstermen, and he was carried to an Ulster dressing station. There are many who disapprove the course of action Redman pursued in politics, but they will at least recognise that he was a man who willingly laid down his life for Ireland and the British Commonwealth.

This morning we are again on the march and eventually arrive at Passchendaele Ridge where we bivouac. Stewart Royle assists me in putting together a shelter. He has been out of action for a time, having been given a job on the company cooker, but was restless and wished to be with the boys, and here he is, having obtained permission to rejoin the company. It is a cold, dark night, and we are hungry, as our rations are inadequate for our needs.

Royle decides to scrounge some food, and leaves for St. Julien where he says the transport wagons are. He will not hear of my joining in the search, as it is too dangerous, and he knows the road well, having served in the Salient two years.

I keep a miserable lonely vigil, for the night is as black as ink and I am completely isolated from the other men of my company. I cannot hear a sound save the distinct thunder of the guns, and an occasional shell as it plumps with a bang nearby. The uncomfortable feeling that I am the sole survivor in No-man's-land creeps upon me. I am alone in a black hole: nothing to see, no-one to talk to: inky blackness and mud and the sound of the frequent detonating of high explosives. The cold is intense, and I can only shiver and wait for Royle's return. It would bring a little comfort to my feeling of loneliness if I could afford a light, but a few inches of candle is all I possess, which I must preserve in readiness to welcome Royle.

Will he escape the shell-fire? I wonder.

I have no sense of time and after what appears an eternity—actually about three hours—I hear the sound of someone groping, and the squelching of feet in the mud. Royle calls, and I light the stump of candle, at the same time murmuring a prayer of thankfulness.

He has been round the Army Service Corps lines, and the fruits of his hazardous adventure are a tin of salmon, a tin of tomatoes, and four ounces of bread.

Royle interests me with the telling of his experiences in Flanders, which takes us far into the night. He has learned to look upon war as an adventure; nevertheless he has confided that the actual motive which prompted him to join us in the line is the greater possibility of becoming a casualty and a blighty case. Death he does not desire, and although unafraid of the worst, the thought of premature death is inconsistent with his idea of life, for he has many years to look forward to. He is full of vitality, and life means much to him: so much, that he wants to get out of this mess with a blighty wound. He is risking death but, being a gambler, is content. Religion has no interest for him, for he believes it to be a pleasant pastime for women to indulge in; yet if he were called to decide upon certain death for the sake of a human being or for the honour of the Empire, he would willingly relinquish his treasured hope of England, home, and all the joys of life he craves: he would give his life, not because it is heroic, but because of a finer feeling within him, a deep-rooted affection for mankind. His brother was killed at Ypres in 1917, and Royle buried him. During the retreat in March last, he threw over two hundred Mills hand-grenades in one day. He has gone through hell and is fearless in so far as he is able to control his emotions and to inspire others: for no man living out here is absolutely free from fear. He is but twenty-three years of age, although his face with the skin drawn taut makes him appear older. We have all aged. A few hours under shell-fire will age any man.

A crump outside causes the earth to vibrate, which puts out the candle. I fall asleep.

My first thought on waking this morning is food. Although still dark, the company is astir, and I long for home and a hearty breakfast and a comfortable fire. We have a meal of a kind, which is far from satisfying, and make our ablutions as best we can using shell-hole water.

'Look!' exclaims Royle, pointing to the sky where a number of tiny balloons are floating downwards. One drops near to us, scattering pamphlets. They are love-letters from Fritz, telling us he is fed up and wants peace. As we read, a German plane darts over the ridge, and sends four Belgian OB's blazing to the ground, while the observers parachute to earth. We attempt to get the plane with a Lewis gun, but fail. An engineer in an old German trench is working a German machine gun furiously and suddenly the plane crashes, hit by machine gun bullets—a rare occurrence.

To watch the whirling mass dropping swiftly like a stone, knowing that a human being is about to be smashed to a pulp, is far from a pleasant experience, and the elation of victory is completely smothered by finer feelings; a crowd of men scramble forward to extricate the airman from the wreckage and render assistance if not too late. An air fight is an interesting diversion, but to witness a plane crash, whether an enemy or one of ours, is a ghastly sight. But this is war, and we are compelled to do these things or we would be blown to blazes ourselves.

We fall in, and the CO gives a lecture on the *billets-doux* old Fritz has showered upon us. We have not to be careless or slack in any degree, or the enemy will take advantage if we are unprepared. If we go on chasing Fritz as we are doing, the war will not last much longer.

We march off, and in the early afternoon have lunch in a comparatively quiet and clean spot. Bell tents have been erected, and it appears we have been left out of the war altogether, which does not worry us in the least. Inspecting the tents, we find bundles of blankets rolled up: how delightful and cosy these look, for these are the first blankets we have seen since leaving rest billets. I choose a good position in the tent, and dump my equipment.

It is getting dark and we have decided to spend the night here, but Fritz decrees otherwise. The voice of the sergeant is heard shouting, 'Fall in, lads! Full marching order!' and my vision of a comfortable bed fades, for news has arrived that the enemy is holding out at Comines and we are under orders to rush forward in motors.

On the dark road we sit on our packs, and wait for the WD lorries, while the platoon officer drinks rum and tea from his water-bottle. I have nothing stronger than water in my bottle, and with difficulty I restrain myself from consuming the contents, for the shelling makes me frightfully thirsty: it always does. I cannot predict when I shall have an opportunity of replenishing my water supply, and must hang on to the precious beverage for a graver occasion.

Thirty men, plus rifles and equipment, Lewis guns and ammunition, and rations, are packed into a WD lorry, and we speed along through the dark hours, receiving a thorough shaking each time the lorry meets a shell hole, while the petrol fumes from the exhaust percolate into the compartment, making us dizzy.

The old bus stops and we jump out. Higher up the road the enemy is putting up a terrific bombardment of heavy stuff through which we have to pass in order to get to our position. At this point the road is congested: men moving up, others coming down. We move slowly and for lengthy periods stand motionless.

On most nights the eyes soon become accustomed to the darkness, but tonight the sky is sinister in its blackness, and we have not yet been able to penetrate the abysmal gloom.

Northumberland Fusiliers are leaving the line for a rest, and warn us of booby traps and mines. 'Mines are everywhere, Jock,' says one of the Northumberlands. 'It's bloody awful at that corner, and lots of our fellows have been caught. I hope you have better luck, Jock.'

'Be careful about picking up souvenirs, Jock,' warns another man. 'Eight of our blokes have been blown to blazes through one man taking a fancy to a souvenir.'

The Northumberlands move off with the parting injunction, 'For God's sake don't touch anything.'

We press on a little further, and the cries of the wounded stretched on each side of the road, waiting for the ambulances, adds to the horror of the situation. We are going into it again, this time without bearings and in the dark, and I feel anything but comfortable.

'If we get through that barrage,' says Royle, 'it'll be a bloody miracle.'

The miraculous happens and my platoon, at least, scrape through unhurt. We take up a position I know not where, and can only keep on guard and trust to luck. Luck is ours, and we escape the worst, although the shelling has been terrific the whole of the night.

10

The Victory March

With the coming of the dawn we find ourselves on the banks of the River Lys. The shelling has abated, and we take the morning air. Breakfast is produced from Lord knows where, in which three Lovat Scouts join us. They have been scouting throughout the night, and have not seen any sign of the enemy between us and Comines. These three fellows have apparently been nosing after the enemy with no means of defence other than a service revolver. One of the Scouts carries an instrument I have not made the acquaintance of before this minute.

'What is the gadget for?' I enquire, looking curiously at the instrument.

'This gives the exact position of the enemy guns.'

'How?'

'We wait for the crack of the Hun gun and the sound is recorded on this instrument; from that we can calculate the distance and position.'

'A pretty fine thing to be mooning about without a few Lewis guns to look after you,' I say. 'What will happen if Jerry finds it?'

'Have no fear of that,' says the Scout. 'Only one of these things has been lost, and that one was smashed up.'

I am mystified with this new invention; it might be as the Scout says, but on the other hand he may be pulling my leg. He appears to be sincere—and I know it is not a telephone.

After breakfast the Lovat Scouts prepare to continue their explorations. 'Best of luck,' I say. 'I wouldn't like to be sniffing Jerry's heels a mile in front of anyone else!'

'We're getting more fun out of it than you poor devils,' says one of the Scouts. 'You can't use your wits against shells. We can. It's wits that count with us.'

I have a feeling that the Scouts are right.

I am detailed to take a message to the company SM who has his HQ about half a mile further back. I find Company HQ in a huge German bomb-proof structure, and enter a building which the Germans have fitted up with luxurious baths, beautifully tiled. Running along the top of the tiled wall is a hand-painted border depicting a kiltie in retreat, with a German bayonet dangerously near his upturned kilt. I am pleased to observe some Germans have a sense of humour.

We cross the Lys on a pontoon bridge made of duckboards supported on petrol tins as floats, an ingenious device erected by the engineers.

A stretch of open country lies before us, and in the branches of the surrounding trees are platforms which have been built for German snipers.

Arriving at Comines, we find the town has been captured by troops in front of us, and we have an easy march during the day despite the fact that we carry full marching order. The mud is left behind, which is a wonderful comfort, and the roads are good. It is interesting to march through villages almost untouched by shell fire, although we do not see any inhabitants, for the villagers are no doubt hiding in the safety of their cellars. The wayside shrines are in a measure consoling. Some have been damaged by stray shells, but most are untouched.

Many people are apt to condemn such reminders as savouring of idolatry. Perhaps this is because images have in the past been adored by the superstitious. I cannot imagine any of our fellows being moved to adoration of a piece of wood, but as reminders, they certainly do help some folk considerably in their private devotions.

Being here amidst life and death, and living constantly with all sorts and conditions of men, we learn a lot about the other fellow: his habits, character, point of view—often the opposite to one's own—and we learn to think more fairly than we do in civil life.

How my mind has been wandering! I suppose it is the monotonous tramp of boots.

The air is still, and the sun is setting as we approach a village. I believe we are to rest here, for most of us are now ready to fall out by the roadside in the last extremity of fatigue, for we have marched at a steady pace of three miles an hour with full equipment. We are about to turn into the village when old Fritz greets us. This is one of his prepared strong points. *Tatta-rat rat, rat, ratatata. Sweese weeze seese weeze. Rat-rat-tat.*

I spy some luscious blackberries in the hedgerow, and although the enemy gunners are active I decide, foolishly, no doubt, to pick one or two of the large berries. I succeed without getting bowled over. We take cover in the hedge, and as the enemy artillery is trained on the road, and a barrage of heavy shells detonate with fearful concussion, we change our position, and jump over the hedge and start digging-in in the open field. We dig feverishly with our entrenching tools, working in fours, and in record time excavate a cover two feet deep.

The shelling becomes more intensive, shell-fire being concentrated upon the field as well as the road, and shells are bursting dangerously near. An officer approaches and says to me: 'They're going to counter-attack.'

'I don't think that at all likely, sir,' I reply.

'He's going to counter-attack. That's what he's putting up the barrage for,' reiterates the officer.

I have no recollection of having met this officer before. He does not belong to my company, and as only my company are in this section, he must have strayed from his own men, or else one of the fresh drafts. I do not think much of his surmise anyway. From my observations of the past hour, old Fritz is getting up steam and is preparing to get away by train. About an hour ago I observed smoke rising in this direction, and wondered if Jerry was burning his stores before evacuating. An enemy plane has also been encircling this area for some time and has no doubt made signals to the artillery to blockade the road to give the rearguard time to clear. I share these thoughts with the officer.

'I don't think he will counter-attack, sir; he seems too busy covering his retreat. Look where the shells are falling, sir. They form a cordon round the village, making the approach impassable.'

'None of that,' replies the officer. 'At the far end of this field is a German trench. Take a Lewis gun there. From that position you will have an excellent field of fire.'

I am not at all happy at this prospect: 'If he has a trench there, Jerry is sure to put his guns on it, especially if it has a range of vision as you say.'

'Go with these two men and post a gun in that trench,' orders the officer most impatiently, which renders it useless to argue with him; disobeying an officer under fire is a most grave offence. I have no alternative but to sally forth, which we do with a snake-like movement on our stomachs. After covering about twenty yards in this fashion, I call to the other two: 'Stop. Kiss the earth and keep perfectly still. I'm damned if we're going into that trench without the officer.'

We lie flat against the ground with no cover from the bursting shells.

'Watch that bloody trench go up,' I say, 'then we can return to our hole.' In a few seconds the trench is shelled, and I am proud of my far-seeing abilities. 'Come on, lads!' I shout.

I cannot imagine what possessed me to argue with an officer. I must have acquired the mantle of Corporal Edwards and started to act as he would have done had he been with us.

When we arrive at the funk hole we have dug, the officer is not to be seen. Puzzle! Who is the officer? Either he is a Jerry in disguise or an inexperienced fool, and I will report the incident to my platoon officer when I can get hold of him.

This intensive shelling continues for nearly six hours, but as far as I am aware none of our men have been wounded. After midnight things are quieter, and another regiment arrives and fortunately challenge our rearguard in the correct military form and withhold their fire, for they had mistaken us for the enemy.

The village is cleared, and the other regiment go ahead, leaving us in occupation of the place. As we have not had a sleep for two nights, and have marched for two days, rest is soothing.

We sit down to a hearty breakfast in the shelter of an underground arsenal. There are several of these structures in the village—long brick buildings with concrete roofs covered with growing grass so as to be invisible to the eyes of prying airmen. The place is packed with boxes of German stick bombs, and we use the boxes for seating accommodation and for tables. We smoke, not giving a thought to the fact that the store contains sufficient explosive to blow us to the moon.

'Look!—twa lassies!' exclaims one of our men who is standing by the open door. This is the signal for a general stampede, and coming down the road are two young women escorted by a British soldier. It seems almost incredible, for we have forgotten that girls exist on this planet.

'They're beauties!' exclaims one fellow. Another answers, 'The taller one's a peach, but the little one squints.'

The Victory March

'I wonder where they've come from?' enquires another.

'God knows,' says the first. 'But there must be more where they come from.'

'I wish we could get a move on,' says the lance-corporal, thinking of the girls.

'I don't!' interposes Craig who has just come to the door. 'When we do move, you can bet your life it is blighties or other nasty things we'll find, and not damsels.'

Lunch is served, which is the usual bully stew and boiled rice. 'What's this, Charlie?' says Cameron who has just received his helping of stew.

'Soup,' answers Charlie, the cook's mate.

'And to think we've been marching through soup these past few months,' laughs Cameron.

It is the will of the higher command that we occupy the village for the night. 'The blokes in front of us are evidently held up not far away,' says the lance-corporal.

'And if that's the case,' I add, 'I can foresee a few pieces of iron coming our way.'

During the night the village is blown into ruins, but we are safe and snug in the bomb-proof shelters generously provided by Fritz.

Dawn breaks, and there is every prospect of the continuance of fair weather with a reasonable amount of sunshine. In the early morning we move forward. The sight of the green fields is refreshing, the country looking even more lovely than it is, for we have seen nothing but mud for what appears an eternity. We march along undisturbed by a living soul. Occasionally a shell splutters into the ground as a reminder that the war is not yet over.

Towards evening we halt in a village where the inhabitants, being less timid, are waiting to welcome us. I cannot see any men: only women and children. We are to billet here for the night. The estaminet is open, but the beer is sour and unpalatable, and the first few men who have obtained drinks express their disgust vehemently, with the result that the others keep their money in their pockets.

We billet in a mill, the machinery having been confiscated and transported to Germany because the people refused to work for the Germans. I hear from the women that the men have been taken to Germany as a punishment.

March to Armistice

Two-tier German army beds cover the floor space of the mill. They are made of wood, and provided with a palliasse made of the paper cloth similar to the material German sandbags are made of: filled with straw or shavings they are not uncomfortable. Hun planes have been sighted flying in our direction, and we extinguish all the candles. And so to sleep.

In the morning we find a plentiful supply of water. We clean our boots and buttons as best we can. I have found that tooth paste makes a good polish for buttons, and have managed a shine to my boots by the application of soot from the tea dixie. I have moistened a brush, applied the soot, and after a deal of hard work have produced a shine.

We gladly make ourselves as smart as possible, to impress the inhabitants that we are the best regiment in the British army, but the psychological effect is even more permanent, for we feel mentally clean, fresh and alert. It is a beautiful morning, fresh and dry, and shortly after six o'clock we set off on another day's adventure. How much more cheerful now that the trenches and mud are left behind. When we meet the enemy in the open we can engage him like men. In the trenches we had to run about like frightened rabbits, dodging high explosives with no means of retaliating: just waiting for death, as it were. Here we have a fighting chance.

This morning the curé and two lay brothers bid us adieu. As we pass through small villages, sometimes less than half-an-hour after the last German has left, the women line the footpath and cheer and wave miniature flags. These people, fed on German propaganda for four years, believe we are starving, and that we are using women soldiers. Peasants run from their houses with bowls of coffee which they hand to us as we march along. Many ask awkward questions, and exclaim 'Monsieur? Monsieur?' wondering if we kilted men are indeed women. We assure them we are *hommes* for don't we know it! Our rail transport in France has always been cattle trucks labelled 30 *hommes*, 10 *chevaux*. As more than ten of us invariably entered a cattle truck, we naturally concluded that *homme* was French for man, although at times we felt almost certain that we must be mules.

Flags are flying from the windows of the houses, and we feel proud of ourselves as the women applaud and hang on to us as we march with chest out as if we were the Guards taking over duty at Buckingham Palace.

The Victory March

At noon we arrive at a place which someone says is Bethlehem, but not having a map, I am unable to verify. I only know that the place is not unlike the other villages we have passed through. The Germans evacuated the village just over an hour ago and we, not wishing to engage them at present owing to the possibility of women and children being involved, halt for a rest and lunch.

After the meal we make a tour of the village and converse with the natives. We listen to stories of the Hun oppression, but of course this is war, and the only real complaint is probably the military discipline enforced by the enemy army of occupation. Nearly all metal has been carried away to the German iron foundries; even the brass candle-holders from the pianos have been confiscated and sent to the melting-pot. Is it possible to imagine the sweet-toned bell which has served for years to call people to church, being used as a casting for high explosive shells? Everything man-made is being sacrificed to war.

Most of our men have been in the church. I am surprised to find so many of our boys kneeling before the altar. This is my first visit to a church—the first opportunity since leaving Etaples, and I find the atmosphere and sanctuary refreshing.

During the march we have not had an opportunity of replenishing our supply of cigarettes. We purchase some from a local shop. Horrors! They are German things, or worse, and are impossible to smoke. *Les garçons*, however, do not despise the fearful stuff: these Belgian boys have apparently acquired the habit of smoking the day they discovered they were able to walk.

'Come on lads—a fight!' calls one of our fellows, pointing to a crowd at the bottom of the street. We arrive at the scene of conflict to find two women scratching and clawing at each other like wild animals, now biting and kicking, hair flying and we are unable to approach to make peace—not that I have any intention of doing such a thing, for I might get hurt. One of the officers orders two men with fixed bayonets to push forward, and this acts as a deterrent and the fighters disperse. I hear that the red-haired woman has been friendly with a German officer, and it will be better for her if she departs from the village at once.

Having settled the women, we are called upon to deal with the boys who are making a stir in the square. They are sending up Véry lights, and exploding detonators with pieces of stone, and the village square resembles a battlefield. We confiscate these dangerous fireworks which Jerry has left behind.

March to Armistice

We receive orders to advance. The three hours spent in the village have been interesting, and it is with light hearts that we prepare to move forward. The Wiltshires enter as we march out, and they give us a rousing cheer. It resembles a burlesque setting from Gilbert and Sullivan as we march through the village. We are decorated with flowers, and in the spouts of our rifles we carry miniature flags of Belgium, the parting gifts of the people. Here we are, chasing Fritz, and halting for a spot of fun to give him time to leave, then continuing with our weapons of defence dressed up with black, yellow and red bunting.

As the village recedes into the distance, our rifles become more businesslike. We continue to wear the flowers in our tunics although this is an improper decoration for a soldier, but as the old soldier says very often these days, 'The army is not what it used to be in the good old days. These civilians are making a mess of things.'

Our forces are gradually surrounding four German armies, keeping old Jerry on the run night and day, while we rest as much as possible. The weather is ideal, sunny and dry, although it is cold at night. It appears that we have left all the rain and mud behind; if we continue advancing at this rate, we ought to be in Germany before Christmas. But I do not intend to be boastful: the Germans were going to be in Paris one Christmas and have their Christmas dinner in London the next. Accidents will happen to upset the best-laid plans. Once we reach the German frontier the war will be all but over, for the Germans will not care to have their towns blown up and before they suffer that indignity they will surrender and seek peace.

Every bridge either under or over the railway has been shattered by charges of high explosive to hamper our advance, but we are not unduly hindered and continue to keep up the pace. The railway lines are pieces of twisted metal, and here and there appear yawning chasms. The enemy is evacuating in such a frightful hurry that he has not the time to mine many roads, neither has he yet found an opportunity to halt his artillery and shell the roads. At intervals one or two shells have detonated, but we have no cause to worry. Canadian engineers are attached to our division, and they are re-laying over a mile of line each day, including the buttressing of bridges, which is considered exceptionally quick work.

In the afternoon we halt in a country lane flanked by turnip fields. From this position the town of Lille is visible, which is still in enemy hands; I should not be surprised if we encounter some of the enemy in retreat from that town before long. Now that we have outflanked him, the time is at hand when we shall meet again.

I rest under the hedge and ponder over the exquisite calm prospect of the landscape. The factory chimneys of Lille in the distance come up hard against a grey-blue sky. In normal times these tall giant masses would have spoiled my view, but now they speak a message of life to be and of peaceful industry, for it is an eternity since I have seen anything man-made which was not shattered beyond recognition.

The wintry sun is shedding a kindly light on the fields, but I rouse myself from this delight, for there is much to do with an enemy continually holding out at prepared positions. Together with others, I raid the turnip field, but to my disgust the vegetables are woody and utterly unpalatable; as we scramble back over the hedge a whistle is blown to fall-in and resume our journey.

On we push, though Muscron, which is deserted, or so it appears, for the people may be living in their cellars in fear of another Ypres. We do not stop to make enquiry, although the engineers work overtime in spotting mines. The engineers are like naturalists rambling in the country: they seek signs and find them, they seem to smell mines as the naturalist smells the nest of a rare bird or discovers an exquisite flower hiding in the moss. They appear to be possessed of an uncanny power, but actually they know the signs and where to look. I do not suppose I could discover a mine in a month of Sundays and, although it is not my job, I would love to be able to locate these dangerous eggs, for to me it is a fascinating game. Muscron is an important railway junction, and Jerry has done much damage with mines.

In the evening we arrive at Herseaux where we are held in reserve, so we billet in the village school. The lay-brothers who reside here make us comfortable, bringing bundles of straw for the floor and fuel for the stove. There would not be much chance for a snowflake in this room tonight, for the stove is glowing red with the intense heat.

The stretcher-bearer has bought a rosary in the village, and in the morning intends to ask the parish priest to bless it in the church. We talk long into the night, for the stretcher-bearer is in that mood for serious talk and we are willing listeners. I cannot say for how long I listened to the stretcher-bearer, for I have been sleeping, and although very early and dark, the sergeant has called us from slumber. In a few minutes the room is a scene of sleepy men groping in the dark for candle ends. Some men rush into the outer darkness armed with soap and towels. I follow into the cold, frosty atmosphere, not wishing to queue up in front of the only pump in the quadrangle.

The moon is still high in the heavens, and the creaking of the pump handle and the splashing of water make an uncanny sound in the comatose atmosphere. It will be three or four hours before the first signs of day appear. If anything is worth while, it is to live in the open and welcome the dawn. Although sometimes only half awake when standing-to in the line, it is a joyous sensation to see the sun rise over the German lines. I suppose at Scout camps I had first gloried in the dawn, and felt that spiritual uplift when the sun was setting. Often at Ypres I have almost forgotten the war and, in the quietness, imagined the singing of the birds and pictured to myself a Scout camp in Derbyshire. Then the picture would fade away as the guns commenced to bid us good morning.

This morning we do not see the sun rise. It is one of those dark, quiet, frosty mornings that you like to listen to when snug and warm in a feather bed; when you hear the patter of feet as an early bird takes the morning air, and you have the pleasure of turning over and continuing sleep before the alarm clock disturbs your dreams. As the cock crows this morning we are preparing for another day: perhaps a comfortable walking tour, or maybe to meet Fritz again.

Breakfast is over and at six o'clock we march off. We get as far as Everignies, as the outskirts of the place are being shelled. The roads are crowded with troops and transports, and we take a narrow lane where progress is of necessity dead slow. We stop altogether and watch the shells burst around the village. An old Belgian farmer is taking hold of my kilt, saying, '*Pantaloon, pantaloon!*' and I hastily reply, 'No. *Alley veet toot sweet.*'

We move forward and encounter more shelling, but do not make contact with the enemy, for another regiment is engaging them.

At night I am detailed for duty on a gas guard at a house which is being used as the QM stores. A heavy bombardment

Outpost of the Argylls on the Lys Canal

Captured German 5.9 near the Menin Road

The Victory March

continues throughout the night, and as the enemy shells whistle through the air and crash with a thundering roar, I feel far from happy, for I am alone except for a dozen or so sleeping men, one of whom snores atrociously, and the presence of these men provides little comfort when I think of the possibility of being wounded without their knowing. The gun-fire appears to be concentrated on the roads and bridges, and the village apparently has not suffered, although at the other side of a small wood, which has been shelled heavily, there is something blazing furiously. Whether it is a church or not, I cannot tell. Our artillery is not very active, owing to the danger of inflicting casualties upon the civilian population scattered in the small villages.

The monotony of my lonely watch is relieved by the sound of feet on the cobbles, and a party of men looms in sight. I hail them, partly because I want to speak to some person, and partly because they may be Germans. They are engineers, who inform me that after bridging the canal three times and having it blown up twice, our men have reached the other side. Two more men come down the road from the enemy direction, and I step out of the shelter of the doorway, and find they are also engineers.

'Hell of a night, Jock!' exclaims one.

'Just a bit,' I answer. 'What's happening?'

'Old Jerry's held up over there and is holding out like hell.'

The other says, 'We've captured three German officers tonight: quite sweet it was. They came along the road in an old car that created a hell of a row as it rattled along on steel rims. I thought it was a blooming new kind of tank, but Jerry has a lot of cars like that because he's run short of rubber tyres.'

The other man interposes, 'They ran nicely into our open arms just like little children, saying they'd got lost.'

'They know where they are now, I expect,' I add with a laugh, feeling much relieved by the healthy converse with human beings. It is surprising what a difference it makes to pass a few words with a person, or even to see a fellow creature, when alone on an outpost.

Towards daybreak I go round to the rear of the house where there is a courtyard and a convent. Two sisters, looking tired, are taking the air, as no doubt they have been in the shelter of the cellars during the night. We wish each other *'Bon jour'* and the ladies enquire about the movements of the enemy. I can only inform them that I do not actually know how near or how far away he is, but assure them the war will soon be over. They smile and, murmuring some words in French, or it might be a prayer in Latin, return to the convent.

After breakfast we march forward again, and the Brigadier General shouts words of cheer.

'On to Berlin, boys! The war will soon be over,' and with this joyful news I lose a little of my tiredness, which however returns as we march on. I never was used to staying up all night.

On we march until at length we enter a village which is being shelled. There is not a soul in the houses, and the Hun gunners are wasting time and scrap iron. My platoon takes over a detached house, and I listen to the clang of the shells as they explode in the empty village. We quickly discover that the village is not entirely deserted. In this house is an old man of seventy-five with his daughter and her little girl of about four years of age. The house has escaped damage so far, as most of the shells are detonating further down the street. A passage by the side of the house is under the observation of an enemy sniper—discovery of which has nearly cost a life. The lucky devil has turned what might have been 'kingdom come' into a joke and is proudly displaying a hole in the collar of his tunic.

On the other side of the street is another danger spot which unfortunately has cost a life. The enemy snipers appear to control the village, and we are not able to locate them. This situation, combined with the painful fact that we cannot see the enemy or his positions from this post, is making us angry, for nothing arouses us more hatefully than does a sniper. We would blow him to hell without any misgivings. We have a Lewis gun mounted in the passage of the house leading to the rear exit of the premises, but there is nothing to shoot save the trees. Another gun has been placed by the front door to command the street, but it is the rear of the house where the trouble will come, if at all.

Our new sergeant is of the quiet and persuasive type, level-headed and cool, and not subject to over-indulgence in strong language, but he has not much experience of actual fighting and is puzzled by the present situation, although the most experienced man would be at a loss to discover the best method of locating the enemy in this region of houses and woodland. Our artillery could easily clear the danger zone, but they have no wish to inflict unnecessary damage.

The Victory March

'I'm going to find that sniper,' says Royle, jumping to action.

'Right,' say I. 'Let's go up above and scout round.'

We ascend the stairs and find ourselves in a loft which covers the whole of the house. From the beams hang strings of onions, and on the floor are sacks of potatoes, flour and other foodstuffs. Facing the rear of the house is a large door which opens inwards, and adjacent to this is a window overlooking the garden. We scan the trees in the background, but are unable to see any signs of snipers' platforms hidden among the branches. The church is to the right and shells are bursting dangerously near; any minute we might expect the steeple to crash to the ground.

Royle leaves his position by the window and goes over to the opposite side of the room to peer through a small window into the front street. To obtain a better view of the woods at the rear I unbolt and open the door, remaining concealed while I do so in case a sniper has the place marked as a target. Nothing happens, so I peep cautiously round the door, and now stand in full view.

Whistle! Crump! Thump! A shell detonates at the bottom of the garden, and I bang the door with great alacrity. Simultaneously something hits me behind the ear, and I gasp as I feel moisture trickling down my neck.

'I'm hit!' I shout in alarm, putting my hand to my neck. Royle is hysterical with laughter, as well he might be, for upon withdrawing my hand, to which a sticky substance adheres, I am relieved to find, not blood, but the innards of a pigeon egg. I fly at Royle and grapple with him, rolling among the bags of flour and potatoes until the fragments of an iron shell pierce the roof causing us to hurry towards the stairs.

Shells now burst in the garden around the house. The concussion, together with pieces of flying earth, break all the windows, so we put up the wooden shutters. A number of these shells are dud and one buries itself actually a yard from the house wall: had it detonated, we should have felt a draught.

Royle and I talk to the old man and plead with him to go, and take his daughter and her baby to safety. The home ties are strong: he does not want to leave his house and says he feels safe with us on the premises.

'What do you make of it, Royle?' I enquire. 'I thought I'd become hardened to the ugliness of war, but I never dreamt that I'd have to hold a post with a machine gun at the back door, and help defend an old man and a baby.'

'No use worrying, Haworth. We've done what we can, but all the same I'd feel easier if the old chap would take the woman and kid away from this.'

The sergeant details three men and myself to indulge in a little sleep. We mount the stairs and enter the loft, and scarcely have I made myself comfortable, than a shell bursts in the garden, and a large piece of iron forces an unwelcome entrance through the roof. At this we discover we are not really tired and make our way downstairs. The baby has been fed with some of our Ideal milk, and is now asleep with her mother.

The members of the section are exceptionally witty and cheerful. This is camouflage, for we are sore in our hearts that these innocent people should be sharing with us what we consider a duty. And folk talk of the glory of war! Here is a sweet little girl who has never seen her father: at the outbreak of war he was called away to defend his country, and she was born under German occupation. God knows where her father is at this moment. Can we imagine the father, knowing his child about to be born, his home occupied by enemy troops, and the only means of communication by short notes delivered through the agency of the neutral powers. In addition, the father is going through the hells of war.

Does the family wish to remain in this house of danger because our being here brings a ray of hope that perhaps a message may come, or maybe the father himself? If that is the reason, the suspense must be terrible to endure.

When will the dawn break? The night is long and dreary.

At last our vigil comes to an end. One of the boys acts as cook and prepares breakfast, not caring what happens if the enemy observes smoke puffing from the chimney: he must get a warm drink for the baby.

The sergeant, Royle and I make another attempt to reason with the old man, and after much persuasion and a threat that we will forcibly eject him if he does not leave, the old Belgian, with tears in his eyes, acquiesces.

The bombardment begins again, and the baby is too mystified to cry. I take her in my arms to reassure her. 'What is all this about?' she must wonder. What part has she had in the affairs of man that these things should happen to her—a child who knows no difference between right and wrong?

The shelling quietens, and the three innocents leave home to

The Victory March

seek shelter in a village further behind, and we hope, out of the range of gun-fire.

I take a peep into the garden at the back of the house. There are several cages containing rabbits and hares, and a piece of ground has been devoted to the growing of vegetables. Through the trees I can see the steeple of the church still being shelled by the enemy. *Crump! Thud!* A shell crashes at the bottom of the garden, and I am in the shelter of the house, with the door shut behind me, with great speed.

The day passes quietly.

A night of waiting and watching. What a damnable business: the house vibrating with the concussion of the heavy explosive shells; the awful feeling of anticipation of the house coming down in a shower of bricks and debris on top of us. By all the rules of shell fire, one shell is certain to get us in the end. And here we are, not able to fire a shot or fling a bomb; we cannot even get out of it.

The night passes; and a morning. About noon we are surprised to see the old man again. He says he is unable to stay away from home, and as his daughter and grandchild are safe, he wants to be with 'his boys' as he calls us.

During the day the enemy are attacked on their flanks, and the position on our front is evacuated, and as night approaches we receive orders that we are due for a rest.

As the platoon leave the house, which is now almost entirely free from danger, except be it a long-distance shell, the old man is seen to be crying. He does not want us to leave: we are his boys. Why cannot we stay with him? The poor old Belgian does not understand that the war is not over for us, and that we must rest in preparation for another assault. He grips hands with each of us, and as we march off, holds up his hand as if speaking God's blessing, and probably is.

Late at night we enter Dottignies, and billet in the convent school. We are to sleep in a dormitory upon real beds, and although we have no blankets, that does not matter.

11

We Will Remember Them

Whizz! Bang! Crash!

In a state of alarm I sit up in bed. Is the building coming down? A moan is heard from the opposite side of the dormitory. I jump quickly out of bed. A light is brought—and lying on the floor is a corporal—dead. The stretcher-bearer stands over the body. I am hardly awake and for some seconds fail to realise the significance of the scene before me. How did it happen?

The major hurries in, accompanied by the captain of the engineers who examine the building for mines. We assure them we heard the whistle of a shell, but there is no breach either in the wall or the roof.

Corporal MacNab of Two Platoon leaves a wife and three children and on the morrow was due for a well-earned furlough to England.

In the morning we discover that a shell had burst in the courtyard, and fragments had been hurled through an open door, penetrated the ceiling and floor, and entered the man's body as he slept.

My septic finger is now beginning to be painful and the last casualty, coming so unexpectedly, is upsetting my nerves. Shells continue to detonate in close proximity to the village, and fear is gradually overcoming me in spite of the mental fight to pull myself together.

In the forenoon we parade on the road outside the school. We are going for a bath. The company officer makes an inspection and all the time shells are bursting behind the school, too near to be safe.

We are restless, as well we might be, and constantly ducking and crouching, and long to seek cover. A subaltern is cursing the inspection and, taking matters in hand, orders, 'Form fours, right, quick march!'

We move off like a shot from a gun, and just in time, for a shell burst on the road where the platoon has been standing. I am in the front section of fours with Royle at my side. We look round as we march, and exclaim the usual things about it being a 'near one.'

Without a warning whistle there is a thunderous crash in front of us. Royle is killed instantly, his head blown completely from his body. Two others are killed, and the remainder of the platoon are wounded. The lance-corporal who stood on my other hand has a hole torn out of his side. The officer who was leading, and myself, are apparently the only two members left standing. I feel something hit my skull, and experience the sensation of feeling something snap in my head. Dazed, my hands go to my head, and finding myself intact and no blood on my hands, I examine my body, for it sometimes happens that a person can be wounded and not notice for a time.

One little fellow, hit in the groin, is screaming terribly, his cries heard above the other groans of pain.

Water is streaming from my eyes and nose, and I realise I am being gassed. I put on my respirator, but still I am inhaling the poisonous fumes. I take it off, and find that a piece of shrapnel has penetrated the breathing tube. With the water still flowing from my eyes and nose I am just in time to affix a First Field Dressing upon the arm of one of the men whose artery has been severed, before he collapses from loss of blood and the effects of the gas.

The other platoon by this time are attending to the wounded, and the corporal joins us, having returned from his course. As he discovers me standing apart from the bloody wreckage he is too staggered to do more than comment,

'Hell! We must have charmed lives!'

He brings a glass phial which contains concentrated ammonia. This I inhale. I can feel myself cracking up completely.

Flowing down each side of the gutter is a stream of blood: gallons of life's blood running into a sewer, each drop representing human energy. I never thought that bodies contained such a great quantity of blood.

We evacuate the convent school and at night sleep in a stable: I say sleep, but that is not possible for me.

After a night of extreme restlessness it is time for us to vacate the stable and enter upon the duties of another day, whatever that might entail. I am asked to take charge of the Lewis gun crew, which means added responsibilities. I refuse.

'What's the matter with you, Haworth?' enquires the corporal with grave concern. 'You're the most reliable and the oldest surviving member of the platoon.'

'Reliable!' I laugh. 'Reliable, with a head like mine?' I say desperately; and after becoming more composed, add, 'I don't shirk the responsibility, Corporal. All the others are new, and it will be an easy matter to take charge of a section now; but I'm not fit. I can't do the job. I know I can't.'

'You must. You and I are the only two left of the old crowd.'

'No, Corporal. In the first place, I've been trained as a signaller, and know very little about a Lewis gun save how to fire and fix ammunition.'

'That's easily settled, Haworth. I'll take you right away and teach you all about the gun and how to repair faults. Come on.'

'I'm sorry, Corporal, but I have, as you know, been under continuous shell fire for over three months, night and day, and yesterday—yesterday . . . If it'd happened in a trench it might not have affected me the same. Those events have shattered my nerves. I feel funky. It'll not be fair or safe for the other men, and that's what we must consider.'

'I didn't realise you'd been knocked up so badly,' says the corporal feelingly. 'Look here, you must report sick at once.'

I go along to a mill, and in a corner of the building the battalion MO has a surgery. The MO is not a British doctor, for the best medical officers are required in the casualty clearing stations, and we must be content with an MO whose chief duty is ambulance work, and who has no concern for sick cases. I describe my condition, telling him quite frankly that the shock of yesterday has made me scared. He places a clinical thermometer beneath my tongue and, after two or three minutes, withdraws it and reads the temperature. I have no temperature: consequently I am not suffering from shell shock, but malingering, trying to funk doing a job. I have never heard of a qualified practitioner taking a temperature for shell shock, but this MO has his own way of doing things.

I am returned to duty, absolutely unfit, all because of a clinical thermometer, and if that four inches of glass was placed in my mouth at this moment, the mercury would rise to bursting point, for my blood is boiling over with indignation.

Such is the verdict, and I must abide by it and make the best of things. I inform the sergeant and the corporal, and their remarks concerning the doctor are unprintable.

The company fall in and march into a field behind the houses, where we go through the exercises of advancing behind a barrage. Very soon we are searching for cover, as Jerry shows us what the real thing is like, and this unrehearsed episode puts an end to our 'playing at war.'

'This village is swarming with bloody spies,' says the corporal. 'Every time we show our faces in the open, Fritz belches shells over like hell.'

It certainly appears that our movements are being communicated to the enemy in some way, but it's difficult to locate the culprit in a place full of inhabitants.

In the afternoon we lay our friends to rest in the village cemetery. The bodies are taken on a ration limber, and a solitary piper pipes a Lament. We march behind, followed by villagers carrying flowers. At the solemn words, 'Ashes to ashes . . .' the enemy sends over more shells which explode just outside the cemetery, and we finger our respirators, expecting gas. I have been supplied with a new gas respirator. A strange thought comes to my mind during the burial service. I find myself repeating a verse from *The Burial of Sir John Moore*, and here, instead of a firing party and a bugler sounding the last post, are enemy shells whistling through the air. I cannot conceive that these bodies, tied up in blankets and lowered into separate graves, are those of men I have known. Though I speak reverently, these bodies are but shells: the real men appear to stand behind, looking on. In each case where I have known men killed, I have been conscious of this unseen presence.

Each of these experiences, though tragic, have helped me to understand the nobility of human endeavour. Out here we see the greatness of man, his courage, loyalty and sacrifice. Mere boys are cut down before they have had an opportunity of putting their learning into practice; young officers fresh from Eton, Marlborough, Winchester, Oxford, and from all the other collegiate schools and colleges—can such an amount of brain power be wasted? We cannot prove that those killed still live on, but we do believe in the greatness of man's mind.

March to Armistice

Today is Sunday, and we have a parade service in the mill: this is the first that has been held since I joined the battalion, and the elderly battalion padre takes it. It is forced, and not at all a meeting for worship but chiefly staged to give the colonel an opportunity of addressing the battalion under one roof: it is more convenient than speaking in the open. The General is also present and at the conclusion of the service says a few words of commendation for the work we have done; he ends with the gentle reminder that we are going into action tonight—I wonder if he is patronising.

'It was all bunkum,' says David Higson, a young fellow of twenty, who has recently joined us from the Trench Mortar Battery. I have known Higson for only a day: he has no love for the colonel nor for the army in general; he is in it very much against his will. As a horse dealer in Scotland, his time has been spent in travelling from fair to fair, and his easy-going life in a caravan is not conducive to army discipline, which he describes as being an infliction upon servile creatures from men who have the whole of the British army system to back them up. He is a dour fellow, yet droll, and his witticisms evoke no change in his stern facial expression.

'Once the army gets you,' Higson continues, 'you haven't a ghost of a chance; it would be a bad thing if the military people had their own way in Blighty as they have out here. You look at the professional soldier. Where is the professional soldier?'

'Well, where is he, Higgie?' I enquire.

'In a cushy job. Directing operations from a safe seat, and letting the poor mutts of civilian soldiers do all the donkey work. The professional soldier doesn't want to get killed. He wants to live on, and retire on pension, to decorate his fat chest with medals like the coat of many colours. He wants to be a colonel, then a general, and then a God knows what. Have you ever heard of a regular officer leading his men over the top? A few of them maybe have the guts, but for the most part, you'll find them doing all sorts of jobs except sticking it out in the trenches.'

'I don't know, Higgie . . . I think you have a pet aversion to army folk in general.'

'I tell you, when the army has a hold on you, it holds fast. There's no sympathy or that kind of sentimental rot. If the army wants men to be killed, it doesn't matter a damn in what condition those men are. If they're dying and yet have the strength to hold a rifle, they're put in the ranks. Nothing can get them out. Why, the doctors are ordered to let no men down if they're able to stand on their feet.'

'Never mind, Higgie,' I say. 'Here comes dinner, and I'm famished.'

I am glad of a diversion, for in my state of mind I am beginning to believe Higson, especially after my treatment by the MO.

As the day is drawing to a close we leave the village of tragic memories, and march forward. After an hour or so we are on a country lane and it is now quite dark. We are nearing our destination, and word is passed down the column for all noise to cease: no talking, no lights. We halt. Higson has attached himself to me. He is a likeable fellow, and during the march has been speaking of his adventures as a horse dealer. Enemy machine guns are trained upon the narrow lane, and bullets now *swizz* and *seez* like a hailstorm as they speed from one side of the hedge to the other, causing us to duck. Although we have received orders to be silent, the colonel gives three shrill blasts of the whistle as a signal to move forward. The air is electrified by whispered curses.

Fortunately for us, the enemy, who must now be aware of our approach, decides to stick to the machine guns, for if Jerry put a salvo of shells in the lane, we should all be blotted out. The machine-gun fire becomes more intensive and, as we have no idea of the enemy position, we must be exceptionally careful.

Our company is chosen for reserve, and we take up quarters in a farm. My platoon take over a cow-house, where we rest and listen to the thud of the almost-spent machine-gun bullets as they splatter against the wall outside. This does not cause any great concern, for the spots of lead have not yet penetrated the thickness of the concrete walls.

The farm is of the usual design peculiar to Belgium, being rectangular in shape. The shippon abuts on to the lane; the entrances facing the farmyard. The farm dwelling is opposite, with a higher structure in the form of a square tower adjoining the house on the right: this is used as a granary, or was, for a party of observers now occupy the highest point, as it has a fair vantage, overlooking the enemy lines. On my left and right, connecting the house and the shippon, thus completing the rectangle, are farm buildings used as stores and stables; the entrance to the farmstead is on my right and separates the shippon from the stables, being in the form of a close, with a store room over.

I am feeling groggy, my head is splitting, and my septic finger is giving awful pain; I have no more comfort than to rest on the stone floor with my pack for a head rest.

Higson, who occupies the next stall, thoughtfully brings me a canteen of hot tea, which is delightfully refreshing.

'Where did you get it from, Higgie?' I enquire.

Higson puts the forefinger of his right hand to his temple, and in his droll manner remarks, 'It's up here where you want it.' He had filled his water bottle with tea before we left the village, and with three stumps of candles has heated it. I go to sleep.

The morning finds me far from well, and my poisoned finger renders my right arm useless. I have it lanced in the farmhouse by the stretcher-bearer, and during this, gas shells burst in the yard and the house is quickly filled with poison gas. We don our respirators and improvise a crude protection for the farmer, his wife and boy. The boy gives me the correct pronunciation of Ypres. Hitherto we have called it 'Wipers' and 'Ye Pray'—both appropriate titles.

The sergeant puts me on the sick list and orders me to rest; he will send me down to hospital tomorrow. Later the sergeant asks me to take a message to one of the other platoons who hold a house in the village. He points out the position on the map and I make my way to the village, keeping close to the hedges, for if the enemy have a field of fire they also must have the area under observation. I duly arrive at the house and find one of the men under arrest. He is a young fellow of nineteen. With no concern for the consequences, he had put forward the hands of the platoon watch one hour.

The officer hands me as many apples as I can conveniently carry: lucky beggars—they have a barrel full of them. I am leaving when two women are brought in, having come through the German lines, and the officer instructs me to take them to battalion HQ for interrogation. On the way Eve relieves me of two of the luscious apples, but I am unable to get them to talk.

The staff are having a meal at battalion HQ and the major takes charge of the women, for rations will have to be adjusted to provide for two more mouths. I hope the major obtains more information from them than I did.

Returning to the farm I find the stretcher-bearer talking to two of our men. A shell crashes in the centre of the farmyard and one of the fellows laughingly exclaims, 'Why did I join the army?'

The stretcher-bearer follows up the remark. 'Have you ever given serious thought to the reason which prompted you to join up?' he asks.

'I don't suppose I have,' answers the man. After a pause he continues, 'I think it was the band. I was listening to a recruiting speech, and when the band marched away, I went with them, and here I am.'

Thump! Crump! Crump! Thump!

We step precipitately into the shelter of the shippon as three high-explosive shells whirl through the air and detonate with a roar at the far end of the meadow behind the farm buildings.

Crump! Crash!

Without warning of approach, another shell drops in the farm-yard and the shattering pieces of shrapnel ring against the brickwork of the tower.

'They're getting closer!' exclaims the stretcher-bearer as we come to the doorway to see better what damage has been done.

'Jerry's trying for the granary,' I remark.

'No doubt about that,' says the stretcher-bearer. 'You can bet your life Fritz knows we're using it for observation.'

'And a mighty good look-out tower it makes,' ventures another of the men. 'I can see the darned thing getting a direct hit before long, and I shouldn't care to be peeping through that window when it happens.'

'That darned strip of bricks and mortar is going to make this farm yard a warm corner, and I bet you don't hear the cock-a-doodle-doo in the morning,' says the sergeant as he comes over to us from the house.

'I bet we don't,' says the stretcher-bearer. 'Everything with wings has deserted this place hours ago and I don't blame them either.'

'If I had wings I'd be miles away from the sound of gun-fire,' I add.

'Well, if this strafing goes on much longer, lad, you'll have wings sure enough,' laughs the sergeant.

The party disperse to perform various duties, and I take my rest as ordered by the sergeant.

March to Armistice

Towards evening two platoons of my company are ordered to reinforce the positions in the line; meanwhile my platoon remain at the farm.

At nightfall I go down with the ration party, for we are short of men. As we return with the rations, an enemy plane hovers above, and as we expect a shower of scrap iron when the enemy gunners receive the signal from the plane, we quicken our steps and break into a lively trot. We have to jump a number of ditches, each between three and four feet wide. It is troublesome work footing it over the soft earth, but unavoidable, for the roads are being shelled, we are being wise and make our footprints among the turnips which is safer but lumpy. Another ditch, and we sling the bags across first and then hop over ourselves. At the next jump something goes amiss: my arm is painful, the sack fails to arrive at the other side and has to be fished out of the water. This incident proves rather amusing, for the corporal is under the impression that I carry the tea and sugar and other perishables, and is quite excited. Fortunately it is the bully beef and tins of milk, and no harm is done.

At the farm the sergeant informs us that every man is needed to reinforce the forward positions, and instead of having a rest in hospital I collect my belongings and march forward. We pass through the village which has been heavily shelled and is still under the fire of enemy machine guns, but where the guns are placed I have no idea. Turning into a narrow lane we find progress barred, for the trees on both sides have been mined and have fallen across the path. Apparently this is the only approach to the post we must occupy, and my section are finding it most difficult to force an opening through the piled-up and interwoven branches of trees. Movement is exceedingly slow for shells are now screaming overhead, and the thought that the enemy shells might fall here is causing me anguish of mind. After an alarming struggle we find ourselves extricated from the wreathing mass, and again on terra firma. Walking a short distance we go through a small gateway into a farmyard. I heave a sigh of relief, because I had been visualising a body twisting through that impenetrable tangle, held in a vice-like grip awaiting the crash of a shell which would not kill outright but would mutilate the body. This is what men fear most: not death, but a body torn without destroying the spark of life.

In the shelter of doorways we post two Lewis guns, each with two men, overlooking the River Scheldt. The corporal and four remaining men of the section, including me, seek the shelter of a substantial cellar: here we are favoured with five barrels of beer, which works out at half a barrel each and half a barrel over. This quenches our thirst, and is less likely to cause dangerous illness than water drawn from the pump.

It is a shocking night for the enemy are hurling hundreds of trench mortar shells from the opposite bank of the river, and the terrific explosions concentrated in one area are playing havoc with my nerves, for I have shell-shock besides the throbbing pain of my poisoned hand. It is a frightful sensation. Hitherto I have listened to shells passing over, knowing they were harmless, but now I get the wind up at the least sound.

We take turns outside with the guns, and the night passes painfully slowly. Our army with the Belgians has come to a halt in face of the Hermann Position which Hindenburg has ordered must be held, and here, on the banks of the Scheldt, we can only hold on.

In the morning the air is still and silent after the violent concussion caused by the trench mortars during the night. The corporal and I venture to explore the farmstead in the hope of retrieving something in the nature of food. The larder is empty so we ascend the stairs to a bedroom, a corner of the wall being exposed to the elements, the result of a shell. We search the room for a souvenir of our memorable visit to a bedroom in the front line when the whistle of a shell sounds, and without further ado we vanish from the room like dew before the morning sun. Bricks fly fiendishly, and with one leap we land at the bottom of the stairs. We go out of the house and meet an officer who tells us that there are no Germans for miles. What a story! I think we have heard that one before. The officer wants us to go through the gate and scout round the river bank, only he does not think it worth while to accompany us. He orders us to risk our necks for nothing, and as the corporal is an expert soldier, we win, for we have no doubt whatever that the enemy is on the other side of the water, and the officer goes back to reconsider, and obtain expert advice.

A guard is posted in the farmyard overlooking the river, and the remainder of the platoon enter the cellar to rest and drink beer. We attempt to fry some pickled eggs that have been found in a jar, but this is far from successful: the eggs must be at least a century old, evidently left by the workmen who built the cellar, and this generation is not having any leftovers. In the comfortable security of the cellar we listen to the explosion of the shells outside and talk of many things.

What prompts men to withdraw a photograph from their tunic pocket? This is a familiar scene. Sometimes it is boastfulness, as a man roughly handles a packet of photographs of girls. There are many men who find an agreeable occupation in boasting of the number of girls who have fallen to them. Usually, however, the men handle fondly the picture of a girl who means much to them—girls who love them; and it helps them to steady their thoughts.

Jock Anderson falls to talking about his girl; his Jeanette was a children's nurse, but her employer took advantage of the girl's love of young children, and little by little added further duties until she was not only children's nurse but head cook and bottle washer.

'The woman was a bloody fool, all the same. Not as clever as she thought,' continues Anderson. On the spur of the moment Jeanette packed up and left. 'Mistress and slave parted,' concludes Anderson.

'Aye,' interrupts Higson, 'until the people own the land and abolish the slavery of capitalism, there'll be no country for free people to live in. What are we fighting for now? We have no blooming castles or land, and we'll get damn all out of this—not even a living wage when this show's over.'

Higson was getting well worked up, although I believe he is too kindly disposed to lead a bloody revolution. He went on to relate how he had tramped the roads and begged from door to door, but always at the doors of the working people. We went on arguing about property and the rich for some time.

'Well, well,' yawns Higson at last, 'I have my way of looking at things, and won't quarrel with you, Chris. I'm going to have a spot of sleep before the night operations start.'

'Not a bad idea,' I say. 'Pleasant dreams, Higgie. Don't let the capitalist system disturb your peace of mind.'

If the war lasts much longer, Higson is going to make us deep red communists. I have already lost faith in doctors of medicine.

At nightfall we man the Lewis guns and console ourselves with the reflection that the enemy trench mortars will not last for ever. It is rumoured the enemy is utterly beaten, but that does not lessen the intensity of the shelling of our lines.

The officer who spoke to us this morning pays a further visit, and informs Corporal Edwards that there is a shell hole opposite the farm gate, and orders him to send out a gun team. He has been observing from the rear, and says we have a good field of fire from the shell hole. This sounds exciting and, as my scared nerves are playing havoc, I volunteer to go out with the gun team, for it often happens that a dangerous venture helps one to conquer that terrible spasm of fear. I feel as windy as a mouse, but I am determined to pull myself together, for the doctor will not help.

Three of us go out. We take every precaution and creep carefully to the shell hole; but we are seen by the enemy and so are unable to fix up the gun: as we are heaped together in the hole, a tornado of machine gun bullets whines and whistles over our heads. Our machine gun corps on the other side of the farm observe the flame from the enemy guns, and return the fire with compliments. What a position! Between two fires. We feel frightfully uncomfortable, for we lie just as we have dropped, and if we move it is certain that a machine gun will settle us for good. For close on half an hour we lie beneath the fire of the opposing gunners when, as suddenly as the firing commenced, it ceases as if by mutual consent and we wriggle ourselves out of the tangle into a posture more compatible with comfort, and prepare to fix the gun.

A figure is crawling towards us from the farm, which we soon recognise as that of the corporal, who calls out to us, '*Allez* back quick' which we obey instantly.

I now feel more in command of myself, and after a rest we take advantage of the quietness and venture forth upon a patrol, for it is rumoured that we are to make another attempt to cross the river, supported by a machine gun barrage. Two attempts have been made without success.

We accidentally stumble across a German machine gun crew on our side of the water, who willingly surrender, saying 'War *fini*.' It is for them.

During the night our patrols surprise a number of isolated enemy gun teams who give no trouble when discovered. Later, our trench mortars send over shattering shells, so full of high explosive ammonal that although the range is local, the concussion produces a demoralising effect upon those in the midst of the explosions. The Machine Gun Corps open out an intensive barrage on our right. The night passes painfully slowly to the tumult of the big bangs and the rattle of machine guns. We are still held by the Hermann defences.

In the early dawn I pass the hastily scooped out trench which the machine-gunners have recently used. It is evident they have suffered the brunt of the German guns, for dozens of packs, saturated with blood, are scattered about.

The mail arrives, and Donald Maclean, who has received a newspaper from home, tells us how the war is getting on.

A message is received that we are pulling out tonight, and fresh troops will relieve us.

It is dark, and as I stand on duty behind a Lewis gun, I wonder if we are as near to the end as we believe. I shudder as I think of spending a long winter out here. It is freezingly cold tonight, and I cannot feel my feet. If this is a sample of the winter, and it is only just beginning, then there will be plenty of work for the 'trench feet curers.' I am wearing as much clothing as possible: winter underwear, leather jerkin over my tunic, great-coat and a thick woollen scarf. Oh for the smell of a fire!

In due course we hand over to the relieving battalion, but not before we have filled our water bottles with ale from the cellar store. The forces who take over our position are happy at the prospect of a cellar filled with barrels of beer, and we relinquish all claim to the home-made brew so long as we are able to leave the place with safety. We take the narrow and difficult path, and again face the ordeal of scrambling through the tangle of torn-up trees. What an unearthly time it takes to cover the short distance.

Arriving in the village square we discover the church in flames, and the red glow is playing upon the stage in time for our appearance. But our role is not that of the chief actors, rather that of the scene shifters who prefer to move about in the dark. The curtain is raised and we must run across to the other side before the audience—old Fritz—looks up from his programme. Ready, go! Will I make it? No!

A trap-door has been left open—a shell hole. Into this I must stumble with the Lewis gun ammunition twisting round my neck, and I am not able to free myself as speedily as I would desire. With beads of perspiration pouring from my brow I jump out of the hole, and my legs carry me faster than they have ever done before.

The platoon is collected and we march away, making a detour to pass behind our artillery. Our first halt is a farm, and the yard is the temporary home for a big gun. The gunners are preparing for action and we are not pressed to stay, nor have we any desire to linger, for the result of a gun being fired is sometimes more nerve-destroying than the bursting of a shell.

It is usual on night marches for the officers to practise map reading in an endeavour to find short cuts. This practice has often been the cause of more bad language amongst the expeditionary force than anything, except perhaps plum and apple jam. The enemy artillery is very active and the shells appear to be following us. The officer leads us down a railway where there is no railway, the permanent way having been destroyed by the enemy to retard our movements, until a large mine crater looms before us, barring further progress. Another halt; another thousand curses; still the whistling of the shells overhead.

After a long consultation with the map it is decided that we must keep to the road and go through a small village; we accordingly about turn and, retracing our steps, strike the road again. As we step on to the road, a volley of shells wobbles overhead, and in a second or two we hear the dull bang of the bursts as the shells fall in the empty village. A terrific tornado of high explosives tears through the air and we cancel all the nasty things we have been saying about the officer, as we listen to the missiles thundering down on the village street.

The officer deliberately took us down the railway to avoid the open roads which are always dangerous at night, and it is fortunate he used some time referring to the map, for although the moments were anxious for us, the time spent has saved us from entering the village at the height of the bombardment. We now feel inclined to cheer our officer for saving us from the murderous shelling.

The shelling ceases and we move forward, and soon hurry through the recently shelled street. At a steady pace we pass by the fringe of the village of Dottignies where we last rested and suffered casualties. Enemy shells have followed us down the roads, and we hear the detonation of more high explosive shells. Tired and footsore—we have not had our boots off for many days—we at last reach the rest billets in the early hours of the morning. This has been a long night, filled with excitement and thrills, part of which I have enjoyed, but not all, for my nerves are not what they were a week ago. Perhaps I may dwell upon the events with a great sense of humour as my mind becomes more normal; but for the present the supreme joy is to take off my boots and socks. Other things can wait.

It is All Saints' Day as we lie down to sleep upon the straw-covered floor.

> And when the strife is fierce, the warfare long,
> Steals on the ear the distant triumph-song,
> And hearts are brave again, and arms are strong.

12

Armistice

We rest at Herseaux for four days, and to our joy the division concert party come up to the village to entertain us.

For four days we drill and salute imaginary officers—why the saluting drill I do not know—and on four nights I visit the entertainment which improves my nerves and drives away most of my fears. I polish my boots with German boot polish, and write letters home using a German lead pencil purchased from the local shop. Who said there was a war on?

On the fifth day we are once more making towards the line. It is cold but dry with a clear sky. I am seized with spasms of sickness during the day, the result no doubt of the last dose of gas, but fortunately we are held in reserve and billet in a village. The officer comes to see me in the billet and informs me I must be left behind and go to hospital if I continue in my present state of ill health. I hope I will, for I have never felt so tired and fatigued as I do now.

The worst happens, for after a rest I feel much better and there is not an earthly chance of being left behind.

I am one of ten men who occupy the front room of a house, and our hosts do not appear to rejoice in our occupation. Before retiring for the night we decide to make a drink of *café-au-lait* which we were able to buy from the canteen when on rest. One of the boys approaches Madame and courteously enquires if she will provide hot water, but Madame is hostile and refuses, so we are deprived of our nightcap.

In the morning we explore the garden and discover boxes of German soda water and articles of German army clothing, some of which we annex as souvenirs. We break up the boxes which contained the bottles of soda water, and proceed to light a fire in order to boil water for a drink. Our hosts, who constantly

March to Armistice

keep a watchful eye upon our movements, observe what we are about to do and become almost frantic with rage. The wood is lighted in the stove, and the old couple continue to run about like the proverbial scalded cats, screaming and gesticulating; but we take no interest. Suddenly the man rushes towards the stove, and putting his hand through the opening at the top, extracts therefrom several pieces of silver, and hastens from the room.

A man from another platoon calls upon us and we tell him what all the fun is about, and he laughingly remarks, 'You ought to be in my billet across the street. The old girl brought us an early morning brandy to drink in bed. She's the goods and looks after us like a mother. Of course, if you blokes were as good-looking as our platoon, things would be different in this house. The trouble is, the old people here don't like the looks of you....'

The remark is cut short by a well aimed boot and, before mischief can be done, Anderson, who has just made the coffee, cries, 'Don't worry, David; have some coffee,' and David, who is always keen on getting something for nothing, forgets about the pain in his stomach.

During the advance we have lost contact with the usual recreational services which have meant so much to men behind the line. This village is dead: not a canteen, no food shops nor houses where eggs and chips may be purchased, for the inhabitants are without food themselves. Our rations have been reduced in order to feed the people living in these villages. We feel abjectly miserable, leading this life of inactivity, destitute of social relations, and all the time the guns can be heard booming in the near distance. The cold, dark night and the shortage of food do not add to our consolation and in desperation I drag Higson on a visit to the Toc Emmas in the hope of affording some degree of distraction from our present discomfiture. After we have stumbled twice into the ditch on the dark roads in the countryside, we find the billet of the Trench Mortar Battery. Their captain is teaching the boys *Rogerum*, a song which, according to the captain, has been the favourite with our brigade since 1915. The song is the story of Dives and Lazarus, put rather crudely but effectively. It is a marching song which has a rich and sacred meaning as we realise how many stout hearts have tramped through those dark days singing *Rogerum*. It is more significant than *Tipperary*, for that is a light-hearted song which has accompanied men on

Armistice

the forward march to the line, while *Rogerum* has been sung by fellows who came down the line utterly wretched, worn out and often wounded.

We return to our billet in time for the rum issue. We are obliged to sleep upon a tiled floor with only one blanket and a greatcoat for a covering. The platoon is astir early, and it is discovered that the pump in the garden has frozen overnight, and we have to break the thick ice before we can wash. Shivers! But what a refreshing warm glow afterwards! After breakfast we parade, and potter about with the guns. The afternoon finds us preparing to march forward again. It is Thursday, two days after Bonfire Night. The big bangs of the war are less pleasurable. A mist is creeping ahead as we march, and ultimately we take over a position in a derelict house. Machine guns are active, and 'minnies' wobble viciously through the air and detonate violently as they strike the ground.

If the enemy has decided to consolidate and hold out for the winter, the prospects are not good. Some fellows believe Germany cannot withstand another winter of warfare, and will throw in the sponge; others think we will soon make another attack, thereby routing the enemy and keeping the retreating German armies on the move until Germany is reached. What then, nobody seems to conjecture, although there is a slogan, 'On to Berlin'; but that city is far from the Rhine.

We content ourselves with holding the position, and do our utmost to confuse and hinder the enemy. Whenever an opportunity affords, we exact retribution because of the insidious 'minnies' he uses against us.

A long dark misty and frosty night passes, followed by a dreary day of anxious suspense. Another night, every moment of which brings a shock to the nervous system as the deafening explosions shatter around our position. Misty daybreak appears, bringing with it the piercing bitterly cold easterly wind. How those men in the early days of the war must have suffered in the waterlogged trenches! Nothing short of a three-mile run will restore warmth to our cold bodies; and here we are imprisoned in a refrigerator. 'I'm going to have a square meal,' remarks Higson, as he removes the lid from a small tin and takes out two lonely Oxo cubes. With the assistance of a Tommy cooker and a canteen of water, the square meal is prepared.

Towards evening a thick blanket of fog springs up, but this

does not prevent the guns from booming, nor the shells from detonating. We rejoice as a battalion relieves us, after we have spent two days and nights in this wretched cold position. We march a few miles and arrive at billets warm although tired and sleepy, and after a meal of porridge and tea followed by an issue of rum, we cast all care aside: stretching ourselves upon the straw-covered tiles we are soon enveloped in precious sleep.

It is Sunday and in the quietness of the village, for once, we realise the distinctness of the day: it feels like Sunday, but there is no church parade, thank goodness, for the atmosphere is too cold to permit spells of prolonged inaction. To keep ourselves warm we indulge in sprinting and springing. The order is given that we are free to go as we please, and I decide to make a social call upon Corporal White, an old friend attached to the battalion signal section. Battalion headquarters staff are housed in a chateau, which is nothing uncommon, for the chateaux have been specially designed and built for HQ staffs. A sentry is on guard at the main gate—a job I do not envy the poor fellow.

'Where are the signallers, Jock?' I ask the sentry, as he comes to the end of his beat and orders arms.

'In the dining-room, but you can't go in this way: you must use the side entrance.'

'I see—the tradesman's entrance. It's a rotten cold job you've clicked for, isn't it?' I remark feelingly.

I find the house has been stripped of furniture, and possibly the owner has not resided here since the beginning of the war. Part of the wall near one of the windows on the upper floor has been shattered by shrapnel, and sacking covers the jagged hole to keep out the winter winds. The signallers are in the dining-room; barren of furniture excepting a box which is described as a table.

'Hello, White!' I exclaim on entering.

'Well, well! Haworth! So it is!'

'So it is, old chap. How are things in your line of business, Corporal?'

'About the same. Still having a cushy time as usual, you know. The signallers always have a good time of it, they say.'

'You don't do badly, anyway,' I say. 'No guards or fatigues when on rest. Any news? We haven't seen a newspaper less than a fortnight old in my platoon. How's the war getting on? It's rumoured among our boys that it can't last much longer.'

'We are near the end, old chap,' says the corporal. 'But—don't pass it on—the German fleet has mutinied at Kiel; Austria has been granted an armistice; and—be careful, old chap—no repeats—the old Kaiser has abdicated and is in Holland.'

'Phew! You're not pulling my leg, are you, White?'

'Quite true! Great news, what?'

'By jove, yes! We'll be home for Christmas after all.'

'Aye! The war's nearly over, but make no mistake—you'll spend Christmas here—or in Germany.'

'Germany?'

'Yes, Germany! We're expecting the Germans to pack in any time now, and in that case we'll march to the Rhine. "The watch on the Rhine" will have a different meaning to the original German. Now, not a word of this to anyone.'

'I'm glad, Corporal. And believe me, this will go no further.'

'Hello, Slippers!' I greet, as I perceive the bearer of this strange name sitting in a corner tinkering with a Don. III. This fellow has been so nicknamed because he has always managed to carry in his kit a pair of slippers which he wears when on rest. 'Well, Slippers, what about a little practice?' I say, as I fondly handle the telephone. I tap out a message at twelves, which is a notable achievement considering I have not used a buzzer for several months.

'I see the corporal has been giving you the news,' says Slippers.

'Yes, it's great!'

Lieutenant Hodgson, the Signals Officer, enters the room, and serenely cries, 'Carry on!' as the other occupants of the room stand. As he becomes conscious of my presence he exclaims, 'Morning, Haworth. How's the world using you?'

'Very well, sir, but I'm still awaiting that vacancy in the signal section, sir.'

'Yes, I've not forgotten, and I expect to be sending for you soon.'

'Thank you, sir.'

'Come and look over the house, Haworth,' says Slippers as the officer converses with the corporal.

'Not much to see, only lousy blankets and 'chatty' men, but it must have been a fine house at one time.'

We go from room to room where we are greeted with friendly

remarks as we look in on the occupants who are in various stages of delousing. Lastly, we enter the guard room which is situated at the front: here the stove in the centre of the room is aglow, fed with branches of trees which flicker and burn brightly. It is a great pleasure to stand in front of a fire, even if it is a stove.

I am loth to withdraw from the warmth, but it is not wise to linger longer than is necessary, and Slippers escorts me to the signallers' room. The officer has left, but has given instructions to the corporal that I have to call at his billet for a copy of the *Green 'un*, a magazine for Scout officers.

I make my leave, and on arrival at the officer's billet I am met by his batman who pilots me into the private sanctum of Lieutenant Hodgson. This house is inhabited, and the room looks exceedingly cheerful with its furniture, pictures and ornaments. In the company of the officer I spend a few pleasant moments, chatting about Scouting, which was his chief hobby before he joined the army. Such is the brotherhood of Scouts: it finds a way of breaking down barriers and equalising men without disturbing the sanctity of rank.

I return to my billet just as dinner is being served, which is the usual bully stew and rice pudding sprinkled with a few raisins in lieu of sugar. In the evening, in company with Anderson and Higson, I go for a walk, and in the next village enter an estaminet in the hope of finding a warm room where we can sit and talk. To our intense enjoyment we find the stove is radiating warmth and comfort throughout the room. We order black coffee, for the beer is sour, and join the other men who are sitting round the stove. The other customers belong to the Manchesters, one of the battalions of pals formed in the early days of 1915. These battalions, composed of members of the professions, clerks, engineers, cotton operatives, miners and the like, drawn from all the normal peacetime occupations, have been almost annihilated: only a few of the original members remain.

Our advancing armies are now mostly composed of boys of eighteen and nineteen, and in peacetime I suppose these fellows would not be doing anything particularly great, and the old folk would be saying the country was going to the dogs. Now, these carefree youths are cheerfully facing up to the hard facts of life, and pouring out their blood for a cause they believe to be right. We have just been talking about the 'March Push.'

March 21st 1918, is a day which will never be forgotten by

Armistice

the survivors. It was hopeless to think of winning the war, and yet something wonderful might happen to save the situation. Under the cover of a thick fog the hosts of Germany swooped down on a front of over one hundred and fifty miles: on and on they came, seven deep. Our gunners were mowing them down, but as the masses fell, others stepped up out of the fog to take their places. We had no supports, no reserves: nothing between our front line and the coast. Bombs, rapid rifle fire which burned out the barrels of the rifles, making them useless, machine guns, revolvers, all poured death into the ranks of the advancing enemy. Our retreat had begun: the war was lost! But—many gallant divisions, represented by the remnants of smashed up companies, held on to the last man—no supports, no reserves, no reinforcements.

'Lads! We stand with our backs to the wall!'

On the enemy advanced, only to be held in check at many points by the self-sacrifice of those gallant defenders. All the training camps in the country were quickly emptied of those boy-men—boys of eighteen.

On Good Friday, the ninth day of the 'push', my camp in Scotland was emptied. I escaped that draft owing to a 'flu germ. I had only recently left the isolation hut. Those cheery lads sang 'Good-byee, don't cryee' as they marched to the station: nine hundred of them, boys of eighteen, going to make the supreme sacrifice. It was heartbreaking to bid good-bye to those I would see no more. It is nothing heroic to say I wanted to be with them: it was the spirit, the comradeship.

Poor Snowball! As he wished me good-bye, the artificial carelessness vanished. We were boys, full of the spirit of adventure, and Snowball was going on the great adventure, never to return: somehow we knew it.

'Perhaps it is napoo fini,' said he, 'but I'll put up a fight for the sake of the "old wife" (his mother) and the girl.'

I knew a good deal about Snowball's girl: he told me quite a lot, especially about the last night they were together before he joined up six weeks previously. My sympathy went out to her. The last letter which he allowed me to read was frank and sincere. She said she would wait for him, and asked that her love should keep him from all harm and temptation. This war has made men and women of schoolboys and schoolgirls. We are old before our time. Youth is carrying a bigger burden than it ought.

March to Armistice

As the train steamed out of the station the boys were singing the old song, 'Good-byee, don't cryee—napoo, toodle-oo, good-byee.'

The YMCA that night was nearly empty, and those who were present were full of sorrow. Those nine hundred boys went straight from home to the battlefield. The call from the front was so urgent that no leave was given. Telegrams were sent to parents asking them to come to camp to see their boys before they went away. Maundy Thursday the camp was full of fathers and mothers—mostly mothers—but Snowball, poor fellow, had no visitors. He had no father, and his mother was too ill to make the journey from Glasgow. He was also denied the parting embrace of his sweetheart.

We return to the billet early on this Sunday evening, and somehow feel that peace is near at hand: nothing is definite, but the feeling persists. All the fellows are talking about the coming peace, and one chap is 'open to bet peace will be signed in a day or two.' Perhaps tonight, says he: all good things happen on Sundays.

We are due to take our turn in the line tonight. During this advance we have been doing easy turns of between two and three days at a time in the line, thus keeping comparatively fresh, and as most of us are well-nigh worn out, a longer spell than three days would be found too exacting, for we have been under constant shell fire. Even when resting we have been in the 'gas alert' area, and from this village we can reach the enemy in an hour's march.

This morning, 11th November, we leave the billet to perform gun exercises in a neighbouring field. On our way we ask an Argyll sergeant, 'Is the war *fini* yet?' and he jokingly answers, 'One more shot to go.'

It is a frosty morning with a mist hanging like a thin curtain. *Bang! Crash!*

'There goes the last shot, lads!' shouts Anderson in great excitement.

We carry on exercises in a half-hearted manner, for the air is quiet—uncomfortably quiet. Our officer has withheld the news of a possible armistice, but we feel as if something is about to happen. Perhaps old Fritz is preparing for a big counter-attack.

Three pigeons fly over from the enemy lines. The drone of aeroplanes is heard, and three British planes, flying low, appear

Armistice

through the veil of mist, coming from our lines. Still the awful quiet. Surely something is about to happen!

We have a rest from our practices, and presently a corporal is seen running towards us, waving his hands wildly. As he comes within hailing distance he calls out with great excitement, 'Pack up, lads! War *fini*!'

And the quietness of the morning is broken by the ringing of the church bells in all the clustering villages in the vicinity.

'Thank God!'

That is all we say.

We observe a momentary and voluntary silence, then shout with joy, and run into the farm-house to tell Madame the joyful news. Then to billets to write letters.

All safe!

The terms of the Armistice provide for all invaded territory to be cleared in fourteen days; all prisoners to be at once returned, while those of Germany are to be retained; the left bank of the Rhine, together with ample bridgeheads, to be occupied by the Allies. Germany must surrender five thousand guns, thirty thousand machine guns, two thousand aeroplanes, together with locomotives, lorries, wagons, barges and other war material. East Africa is to be evacuated; and all submarines, and a large portion of the German navy to be handed over. The blockade is to continue.

Such are the preliminaries before the nations consider any terms of peace. The nation which was once the greatest military machine in Europe is wrecked.

Armistice Night at home will probably be one ceaseless round of riotous jollification, elation and victory: it will provide a safe way of giving vent to the repressed emotions and distressing thoughts which have burned our womenfolk in particular during the long dark miserable days of the war. The sight of the telegraph messenger and the dreaded fear it has caused to surge within the anxious hearts of those who have loved ones in the war zone; the ring of the front door bell at an unusual hour; the terrible anxiety, the torturing suspense, are no more.

The Cease Fire has been an angel of mercy to thousands of brave hearts. To many it has made little difference, since they lost their world when their menfolk were called away so tragically: they remain comfortless, at all events for a season; for with the passing of time, although the scars of affliction will never vanish completely, they will assuredly find peace at last. For others the cessation of hostilities will be a disaster. Little complaint has been made by the men in the field regarding the high wages paid to munition workers, and siege prices paid for ammunition which has brought about inflated prices all round. The men in the field were useless without shells: these had to be manufactured, people had to make them; but those at home were able to sleep in a bed; and the difference between the remuneration of a serving soldier and that of a person on munitions was out of all proportion to the risks involved. Those high prices have been settled in paper currency—IOU's—and the enormous bill will have to be met, and by all, whether all have shared the material benefit or not.

Tonight in our little starving village there is no apparent jollification or festivity: there is no dancing, no music, no spectacular display of squibs and rockets. All is quiet, nervously quiet, and there is no wine in the impoverished *estaminets*. As a contrast to feasting, our meagre rations are being shared with the civil population who are becoming exceptionally fond of army bully beef, although our hard biscuits are beyond their delicate tastes.

The morning after Armistice we parade for a thanksgiving service at which the CO disturbs our peace by remarking, 'Do not think that Armistice means you will be able to return home. On the contrary, it will be months, even years, before you are able to leave. It will be years before the army is demobilised.'

Tactless or ungenerous—I know not which—but the phrase, 'It will be years' is the signal for bitter dissent, and cries of 'Oh!' followed by general uneasiness and suppressed hissing in the ranks, which causes the RSM to bellow, 'Silence in the ranks!'

The battalion march past the CO, and on the command, 'Eyes right!' Higson who is muttering imprecations upon the military people, refuses to salute by turning his head and eyes to the right. The RSM thunders, 'Eye's right!' but Higson makes no response and the RSM leaves the CO, rushes madly to Higson and forcibly turns his head to the right. Company Office for Higson in the afternoon, and he returns smiling, having escaped punishment by pleading that he had a stiff neck and was unable to salute.

With Higson and Anderson I go for a walk in the evening. On our way to the next village a sudden sheet of flame illuminates

Armistice

the darkness of the road, and Anderson excitedly yells, 'Look! The sky!'

A lurid glow is spread over the sky, and as a tongue of flame leaps devouringly skywards and falls downwards again, as if it had nothing to hang on to, we pause for a while. A shower of sparks rising after another sudden glow, tells of something that has collapsed. We stand and watch the glow which waxes and wanes fitfully. Fascinated by the streams of flames and sparks we now hurry towards the next village, making conjectures as to the probable cause of the conflagration.

We break into a run and soon arrive at the scene, which is in the centre of a street. Bitterly surprised, we find a half-demented crowd of civilians hurling furniture and other household effects into the flames. A few English soldiers are standing gazing at the wanton destruction of a home, but are powerless to prevent the frenzied villagers from wreaking vengeance. We discover that the unfortunate householder has been friendly with the Germans during the occupation of the village, and the people are filled with a bitter hatred. The woman herself would have been sent to the flames had she not been safely escorted by a party of British engineers, and placed out of danger.

When the invading German army approached in 1914 these same people were frantic, terrified, and in their misery they implored God to save them: most people do that when in danger of death and oppression, and forget all about their blessings of the past later.

We discover that some of the people are angry that an armistice has been granted. They hate the Germans so much that they are prepared to sacrifice not their own lives but the lives of their men in order to obtain satisfaction of knowing that German towns would be ruthlessly destroyed and German women and children slaughtered. Yesterday, when the dispatch to all stations was read, giving the terms of the Armistice, we realised how much the Allies have gained without the further loss of blood. Germany is utterly crushed, absolutely defeated. What will be the result of the ultimate peace if hatred cannot be sublimated? We cannot have a vindictive peace.

To be fair to the people of this unfortunate country, we must remember that for the past four-and-a-half years they have been living under the iron heel of German military discipline, and at times must have been victims of acts of despotism displayed by

March to Armistice

their rulers which has rankled; and now the victory has come, they are eager in the heat of the moment to exact retribution for the insults they have endured. With the passing of time they will perhaps learn that hatred is not only injurious to themselves but to the peace of the world.

On 15th November, Marshal Foch sends the following message to the commander of the British forces, Field Marshal Haig:

> Your soldiers continued to march when they were exhausted, and they fought, and fought well, when they were worn out. It is with such indomitable will that the war has been won. At the moment of ceasing hostilities, the enemy troops were demobilised and disorganised and their lines of communication in a state of chaos. Had we continued the war for another fortnight, we might have won a most wonderful and complete military victory. But it would have been inhuman to risk the lives of one of our soldiers unnecessarily. The Germans asked for an armistice. We renounced the certainty of further military glory and gave it to them. I am deeply sensible of the fact that Lille has been delivered without damage to the town, and I am grateful for the help given so generously to the inhabitants.